THE ICING
ON THE CAKE

THE ICING
ON THE CAKE

Innovative cakes for all occasions

GREG ROBINSON & MAX SCHOFIELD

BLOOMSBURY

First published 1988
Reprinted 1989
This paperback edition published 1992

Copyright © 1988, 1992 by greg Robinson and Max Schofield
Bloomsbury Publishing Limited, 2 Soho Square, London W1V 5DE

A CIP record for this book is available from the British Library
ISBN 0 7475 1241 8

Origination by Universal Colour Scanning Limited, Hong Kong
Printed in China
Typeset by Rowland Phototypesetting Limited, Bury St Ednonds, Suffolk

The Icing On The Cake
was produced by nigel osborne
115J Cleveland Street, London W1

Art Director   Nigel Osborne
Editor   Linda Sonntag
Photography   Mark French
Artwork   Fraser Newman

CONTENTS

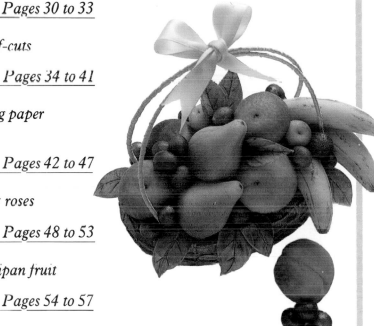

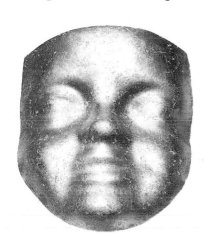

UTENSILS

When buying cake making equipment, particularly cake tins, knives, nozzles and cutters, it really is worth spending just that little bit extra on high quality items that will last you a good many years. Other items such as food colour pens, cake boards and pillars are widely available and of excellent quality and variety. It is worth buying a small work box in which to put all your food colours, piping bags, modelling wire, florists' tape and paint brushes, so as to keep them in good condition.

1 Cake tins
2 Pastry brush
3 Rolling pin and spoon
4 Mixing bowl
5 Sieve and cooling tray
6 Whisks, knives and spatula
7 Icing cutters
8 Icing smoother
9 Pillars, board and candles
10 Tissue paper, foil and scalpel
11 Food colour in jars and pens
12 Skewers
13 Florists' tape 'gutteroll'
14 Icing bag and nozzles

SCALES

Accurate measures have been used throughout the book for weighing ingredients. A set of scales should last a lifetime and it is worth investing in a good pair which will serve all your ordinary requirements.

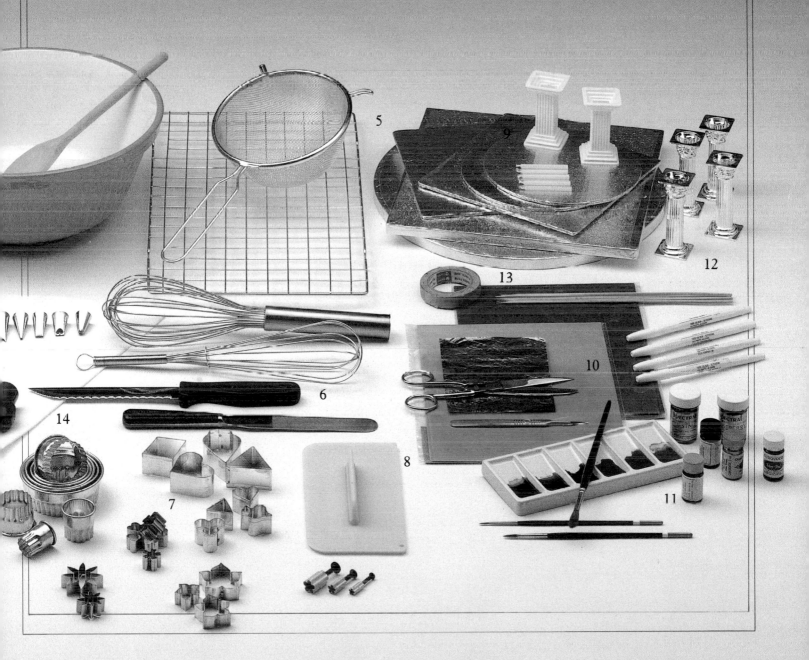

BASIC TECHNIQUES

The cakes in this book have been invented with one aim in mind – to give pleasure, to the decorator as well as to everyone who looks at and eventually eats the cake. Thirty projects are presented. Step-by-step photographs and clear instructions show you exactly how to create everything from a jaded Statue of Liberty to a teddy bears' picnic, all in cake, marzipan and icing.

Some of the cakes demand a degree of dexterity. There is a panda, for instance, sculpted out of three cakes placed one on top of the other. The effect is stunning. Other cakes, such as the crab and the rosette, can be made to look really professional by absolute beginners.

Various skills are taught in this book, among them modelling, moulding and marquetry in marzipan and icing and handpainting with food colours. Learning these techniques and their application will inspire you to invent cakes of your own. Tips and timesavers are included for busy cooks.

There is a cake to fit every conceivable occasion, from Christmas to Valentine's Day. For a wedding, there is a traditional three-tiered cake exquisitely decorated with flowers, or as an alternative wedding cake we offer a breathtaking hot air balloon. The decorations on many of the cakes form gifts in themselves. They may be edible, but they are too good to eat, and they can be taken off the cake before it is cut and kept as a permanent reminder of the occasion.

THE CAKE

A wide variety of cakes can be decorated, not just the rich fruit cake traditionally baked for Christmas and weddings. The criterion is that the cake should retain its shape during and after decorating. You should bear this in mind when inventing new designs or decorating bought cakes.

If the cake is to provide a platform for surface decoration, as with the First Night Cake or the Partridge in the Pear Tree, then any firm cake, including fruit cake, will be suitable. If the cake is to be sculpted, as in the Panda or the gondola for the alternative wedding cake, then a fine and close-textured madeira will be ideal, as it will not break and crumble under the carver's knife. Parkin is another cake that responds well to delicate knifework. Soft cakes too can be decorated – a Genoese sponge forms the basis of our strawberry and cream tea cake and a chocolate truffle cake which requires no cooking provides the basis of a pair of Piscean fishes.

In most cases a cake will rise during cooking, and usually we cut off the resulting dome to make a regular block of cake. An exception is rich fruit cake. This we turn upside down, filling the gap between cake and board with marzipan. The surface of the cake is then perfectly flat and level.

Offcuts of cake need never be wasted. Eat them straight away, crumb them for use in truffle

cake, or use them in trifle. Remember to plan for extra baking time in projects that consist of more than one cake – each cake should be baked separately in the centre of the oven for the correct temperature. We have used size 2 eggs throughout unless otherwise stated.

A final point: many of the cakes featured here have been made big enough to decorate on a generous scale: they will serve quite a number of people. You can of course make your own cakes as large or as small as you wish.

MARZIPAN

The purpose of marzipanning a cake – apart from adding something delicious – is to seal the moisture in. This makes the cake keep longer and provides a firm dry basis for the icing, which should on no account be allowed to get damp.

Marzipan almond paste comes in two colours, yellow and white. On the whole the white variety is additive-and colour-free, but more expensive. Which you use is a matter of preference, though if the marzipan is to be painted, white is best, as yellow does not accept colour so well. Keep marzipan at room temperature and roll out according to the recipe instructions. It handles like pastry. The cake is spread thinly and evenly with apricot jam and the marzipan, usually about ¼″ (5mm) thick, is stuck to it. Be as accurate as you can in marzipanning, as irregularities and bumpy seams are likely to show up on the icing.

ICING

Four kinds of icing are used in this book; each has different characteristics and is used for a different purpose. With the exception of tragacanth, the cost of each is minimal, so much so that you can make up a batch of icing and experiment with the different decorations in the book, and ideas of your own, before deciding which project to tackle.

FONDANT ICING

Fondant is used to cover most of the cakes featured in this book. It handles rather like pastry and produces a soft moulded finish that is easy to cut and does not splinter – unlike traditional royal icing. Fondant remains soft for several hours after application – even fingertip pressure will mark it. It also shows up any irregularities in the marzipan, especially likely round the seams. However, fondant gives a very professional finish and is quick to use after a little practice. Wrap any leftovers in cling film for later use. If it begins to feel rather dry as you roll it out, add a few drops of water and knead until soft and pliable. Sometimes air bubbles may appear in the icing. Prick them with a pin to release the air.

To make fondant icing
1 box (500g) icing sugar
1 egg white
2 tablespoons (30ml) liquid
glucose
cornflour

Put the icing sugar, egg white and glucose into a food processor if you have one, or work by hand. Blend until the mixture resembles lumps of breadcrumbs. Tip into a mixing bowl and knead until it takes on the consistency of bread dough. Add a little cornflour as necessary to prevent the mixture from becoming too sticky. The icing is ready when it no longer

feels sticky and can be rolled out on a work surface lightly dusted with cornflour without sticking. You can use it straight away, though some people prefer to leave it overnight wrapped in cling film and sealed in an airtight container.

GELATIN AND TRAGACANTH ICING

Gelatin and tragacanth are used for moulding decorations, particularly small delicate shapes such as flowers. Both dry very hard. Gelatin is cheaper and easier to make and can be used on all occasions instead of tragacanth. Tragacanth is more elastic and hardens less quickly, but there are problems with making it. It can be difficult getting hold of gum tragacanth and unless there is a good supplier of cake making and decorating equipment near you, you may have to order it in a large quantity from a chemist, which will be expensive. Tragacanth can only really be made in a food processor. Before you begin you should make sure the motor is strong as the icing mixture is very dense and may well ruin a small machine. Tragacanth is delightful to use if you have the resources to make it, but if not, use gelatin, which is excellent for the purposes we recommend.

To make gelatin icing
1 box (500g) icing sugar
½oz (12.5g) gelatin powder
4 tablespoons (60ml) water
2 teaspoons (10ml) liquid
glucose
cornflour

Put the water in a heatproof bowl and add the gelatin. Leave to soak for two minutes. Place the bowl in a pan with ½″ (1cm) water and set on the stove. Heat gently until the gelatin dissolves. Remove from the heat and stir in the liquid glucose. Allow to cool for two minutes. Turn the mixture into a bowl containing the icing sugar and mix in. If the mixture seems wet add a little more icing sugar. Add sufficient cornflour to allow the icing to be worked like bread dough. The finished icing should not be sticky. Wrap in cling film and place in an airtight container until ready to use.

To make tragacanth icing
1 box (500g) icing sugar
5 teaspoons (25ml) cold water
2 teaspoons (10ml) powdered gelatin
3 teaspoons (15ml) gum tragacanth
2 teaspoons (10ml) liquid glucose
4 teaspoons (20ml) white vegetable fat
white of 1 egg

Put the water in a heatproof bowl and sprinkle on the powdered gelatin. Place the bowl in a pan with ½″ (1cm) water and heat until the gelatin dissolves. Remove from the heat and add the liquid glucose and vegetable fat. Stir until dissolved and well mixed. Tip into a food processor or blender with the icing sugar, egg white and gum tragacanth and work until well combined. To begin with the icing will appear almost beige in colour. Turn the speed of the mixer up to maximum for a minute or two until the icing is very white and a little stringy. Put the icing in a plastic bag and refrigerate overnight.

ROYAL ICING
Royal icing used to be used exclusively to cover cakes, but it is immensely hard and brittle and fondant is now much preferred. However, its soft paste-like consistency and quick setting quality make it ideal for creating peaks of 'snow', as in the Christmas Tree, and for piping, as in the Get Well Basket of Fruit. The larger the opening of the piping nozzle, the stiffer the icing needs to be. In this book royal icing is used mainly for fastening decorations in place – it is an excellent edible glue that sets rock hard.

To make royal icing
1 egg white
12oz (350g) sifted icing sugar

Beat the egg white to break it up and add the icing sugar in batches, mixing after each addition. Add sufficient icing sugar to make the required consistency. Cover the icing with cling film, pressing it down gently on the surface to remove any air bubbles. Keep until required, but do not store in the fridge as it will absorb moisture and this will alter the consistency.

CUTTING THE CAKE
First remove the decoration. This can be reassembled and kept as a souvenir. If the cake is square or irregular, cut it in half, then cut the half in slices. Cut the slices into portions. Cut wedge shaped slices from a round cake. In the case of the Champagne Bucket, remove the bottle and napkin and slice the bucket down the seams. In the case of the Valentine cake, lift off the box before cutting.

CORRECTING MISTAKES
● In sculpting, if you carve off too much cake by mistake, either stick the piece back on with jam or replace it with a piece of marzipan.
● If, when the marzipan has dried, you find one of the seams is irregular, fill the crack and round off the edge with royal icing – it will set like cement and make a smooth base on which to apply the fondant.
● If, once the icing has dried, you find a fault in it, disguise this by painting with food colours.
● If you make a mistake in painting, wait for the paint to dry, then paint over it.

ADAPTING ARTWORK TO SIZE FOR YOUR OWN CAKES
The designs for all the cakes can be found on pp. 182-190. Naturally they have had to be reduced in size to fit the pages. You will thus have to increase the size to fit the cake you wish to decorate. You can either go to a photocopying or print shop, where this will be done for you very cheaply to your specifications, or you can do it yourself. Trace out the design and draw a square round it to fit as tightly as possible. Divide each side of the box into ten equal parts, then join the lines from top to bottom and side to side to make 100 squares. Now draw a square that just fits the size of cake you want to decorate. Divide this into 100 squares as well. Copy the design, square by square, from the smaller onto the larger grid. Though you are drawing freehand, you will have reproduced the design exactly.

USEFUL EQUIPMENT
● Graphite paper – like carbon paper – is useful for transferring a traced design on to icing, where it will be painted over. Note, however, that the trace left contains lead, so this method should not be used on anything that is to be eaten.
● As the photographs show, we always use a scalpel for cutting out icing shapes. The fine sharp blade of a scalpel, a modelling knife or a Stanley knife will give more accurate results than most kitchen knives.

FOOD COLOURS

Specialist cake making and decorating shops offer a wide range of food colours, from the light pastel shades best used only with traditional piped royal icing to rich thick paste colours that look almost black in their pots. Gold and silver paints and coloured lustre powders are also available. Though edible, they do have a slightly metallic taste and should not be consumed in great quantities.

You can increase the range of colours in your palette by blending and mixing. Picture 1 shows the paler shades that result from adding water. Picture 2 shows how two colours are brushed together while still wet to create a third shade. Picture 3 shows how pale blue and dark blue are worked together by dabbing and stippling to create the illusion of watery depths – this is the technique used in the Teddy Bears' Picnic. In picture 4 grass is produced by splaying out the bristles coated in green food colour, then lightly stippling over the lines while the paint is still wet. Picture 5 shows the effect that can be achieved by applying colour with an open-textured sponge. A closer-textured sponge gives a softer and subtler effect, provided it is not too wet, as in picture 6. In picture 7 a potato print is demonstrated. In picture 8 we reproduce a wood grain effect. First brush the surface with pale brown and allow to dry. Then drag a medium sized paintbrush, bristles coated in dark brown, along the 'grain', swerving to allow for knot holes – concentric circles of dark brown.

On one or two occasions in this book we have used an airbrush, which allows for a subtle and even application of colour. However, as this is not a piece of equipment likely to be found in most homes, we have always given alternative directions for producing the same effect.

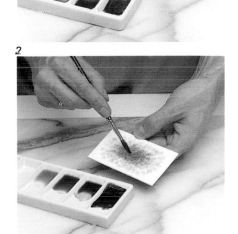

1

4

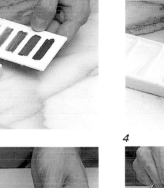

7

2

5

8

3

6

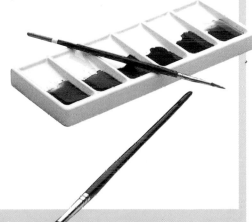

AFTERNOON TEA CAKE

A stencil is a simple and inexpensive way of decorating the delicious moist walnut cake pictured on p. 17. Take the design for the stencil from the back of the book, use a paper doily or devise a geometric or flower pattern of your own. You can make the design more intricate by using a number of colours. Take care to leave one colour to dry before applying the next or you may smudge the outline. This is a versatile decoration that can be used to great effect on any number of cakes.

To make the cake. Mix together the butter or margarine, sugar and syrup, and beat until light and fluffy. Add the eggs one at a time and incorporate into the mixture. Follow each egg with a spoonful of flour. Fold in the remaining flour and the chopped walnuts. Grease a 9″ (23cm) round cake tin and line with grease-proof paper. Spoon in the mixture and level off the top. Cook in a preheated oven at 160°C/325°F/Gas mark 3 for about 1 hour to 1 hour 10 minutes, or until firm to the touch. Check the cake after 40 minutes and if browning too quickly, cover the tin with a double thickness of paper or kitchen foil. Turn out the cake and allow to cool.

For the filling, mix together the butter or margarine and sugar and beat until smooth. Add vanilla flavouring and spread on the split cake.

TIMESAVERS

TIMESAVER If time is very short use only one colour and complete the stencil in one move.

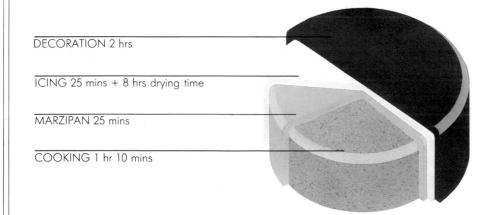

DECORATION 2 hrs

ICING 25 mins + 8 hrs drying time

MARZIPAN 25 mins

COOKING 1 hr 10 mins

INGREDIENTS

8oz (225g) butter or margarine
4oz (125g) soft brown sugar
4 tablespoons golden syrup
4 eggs
8oz (225g) self-raising flour
4oz (125g) chopped walnuts

Filling
4oz (125g) butter or margarine
8oz (225g) sifted icing sugar
vanilla flavouring

Decoration
1lb (450g) marzipan
1½lb (675g) white fondant icing
apricot jam

Equipment
food colours
ribbon
thin card for the stencil

2 Using the design on *p.182* trace out the stencil pattern on to a piece of greaseproof or tracing paper. If necessary increase the size of the pattern to fit your particular cake. With graphite paper transfer the design on to thin card. In this photograph the stencil has been divided into four sections to allow for the use of an airbrush with four different colours. However, if a paintbrush is being used, do not divide the stencil. With a sharp knife or scalpel, cut out the stencil pattern.

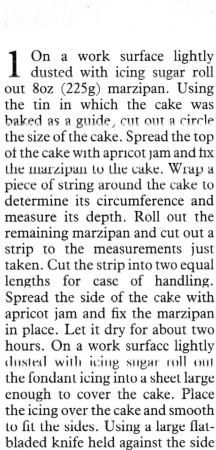

1 On a work surface lightly dusted with icing sugar roll out 8oz (225g) marzipan. Using the tin in which the cake was baked as a guide, cut out a circle the size of the cake. Spread the top of the cake with apricot jam and fix the marzipan to the cake. Wrap a piece of string around the cake to determine its circumference and measure its depth. Roll out the remaining marzipan and cut out a strip to the measurements just taken. Cut the strip into two equal lengths for ease of handling. Spread the side of the cake with apricot jam and fix the marzipan in place. Let it dry for about two hours. On a work surface lightly dusted with icing sugar roll out the fondant icing into a sheet large enough to cover the cake. Place the icing over the cake and smooth to fit the sides. Using a large flat-bladed knife held against the side of the cake, trim off any excess icing. With a plastic sheet, smooth the icing on the sides of the cake to produce a neat finish. Allow the icing to dry for eight hours or overnight.

3 Choose your colours and decide which sections will be painted with which. Lay the stencil on the surface of the cake. Put some colour on your paintbrush without making it too wet. Gently brush over those sections of the stencil you wish to colour first. Of course the whole stencil may be painted in one colour, but if using more than one, there are two ways of proceeding. If you are neat in your painting it is possible to paint the whole stencil with several col-

ours in one process, but keep it as free of smudges as you can to avoid colours 'straying' to other sections and mixing with other shades. If you are not confident of doing this, remove the stencil after you have applied the first colour and allow to dry for at least an hour. Wipe the stencil clean with a tissue. Reposition the stencil when dry and proceed with your second colour. Continue in this way until you have completed the design.

4 When the stencil is complete and has dried, you can add further detail should you wish to, such as small highlights in silver or shadows in a deeper shade of one of your chosen colours. Do not attempt this if you feel you may spoil the effect.

5 Stencils are available in many large stores in response to a renewed interest in craft and individualized interior design. You could select a bought stencil of the right size instead of using the design on *p.182*, or you could use a doily. Carefully pin the doily of your choice to the surface of the cake, being sure to count all the pins and take them out afterwards.

6 Apply the paint in the same way, being careful not to break the delicate doily. Do not overload the brush with colour. You can paint the whole design without removing the doily. If you do need to remove it between colours, use a fresh doily of the same design rather than trying to wipe the first one clean.

7 When the design is complete, you can tidy up smudges with a paintbrush, or indeed add further detail.

ALLEY CAT

The dustbin is made from three 6" (15cm) round chocolate chip madeira sponges with a chocolate fudge filling. The 'rubbish' is sweets, which makes the cake ideal for any children's party – if time allows, you could make icing 'rubbish' to go inside the dustbin, such as tin cans, bottles, an old TV set and a few fishbones. The cat is modelled from marzipan. This cake offers plenty of scope to anyone handy with a paintbrush. The finished cake can be seen on p. 23.

To make the cake. Grease a 6" (15cm) round cake tin and line with greaseproof paper. Cream together the butter or margarine and sugar until light and fluffy. Beat in the eggs one at a time, followed by a tablespoon of flour. Sift the remaining flours together and fold into the mixture, followed by the lemon juice and chocolate chips. Spoon the mixture into the tin and level off the top. Bake in a preheated oven at 160°C/325°F/Gas mark 3 for about an hour or until firm to the touch. Cool in the tin for 5–10 minutes. Turn out of the tin and allow to cool on a wire tray. Cut each cake in half to sandwich with the chocolate filling.

To make the filling, put the chocolate and butter in the top of a double saucepan or in a heatproof bowl over a pan of gently simmering water. Heat until the chocolate melts. Remove from the heat and beat well until smooth. Beat in the egg yolks and sufficient sugar to give a thick smooth spreading consistency. Allow to cool slightly and use to sandwich the cakes together.

TIMESAVERS

TIMESAVER If you would like a less pristine looking dustbin, miss out the vertical marzipan strips and concentrate on giving the bin a more battered appearance suitable for a back alley.

TIMESAVER To simplify the colouring of the bin just add a little black food colour to the icing and knead to produce an even grey. A few highlights can then be added in black or silver.

TIMESAVER The marmalade cat is quite easy to make, but you could use a bought marzipan cat or a favourite toy instead.

DECORATION 2 hrs
By simplifying the decoration as above, up to 1 hr 45 mins can be saved.

ICING 45 mins + 5 hrs drying time

MARZIPAN 1 hr 30 mins

COOKING 1 hr per cake

INGREDIENTS

Cake (for one cake)
4oz (125g) butter or margarine
4oz (125g) caster sugar
2 eggs
4oz (125g) self-raising flour
2oz (50g) plain flour
2 teaspoons lemon juice
6oz (175g) chocolate chips

Filling
8oz (225g) plain chocolate, broken into pieces
4oz (125g) butter
4 egg yolks
8oz (225g) sifted icing sugar

Decoration
10" (25cm) round cake board
1lb (450g) white marzipan for the cat
1lb 8oz (675g) yellow or white marzipan for the dustbin
1lb (450g) fondant icing for the dustbin
8oz (225g) gelatin icing for the dustbin lid handles
sweets
apricot jam
a little royal icing

Equipment
food colour
modelling wire

1 Spread the chocolate filling on the cakes and sandwich them together. Measure the height of the cake and, using a piece of string or cotton, measure the circumference also. Spread the top and sides of the cake with apricot jam.

3 Once again, measure the circumference of the cake. It will be slightly bigger now, because of the layer of marzipan. Roll out the marzipan and cut out two strips ¾″ (2cm) wide and long enough to go around the cake. Spread the strips with apricot jam and fix round the top and bottom edges of the cake.

2 Roll out the marzipan and using the base of the tin in which the cakes were cooked as a guide, cut out a circle of marzipan and fix on top of the cake. Roll out the marzipan again and cut out a rectangle according to the height and circumference measurements already taken. Fix to the sides of the cake.

4 Measure the distance between the two strips of marzipan just applied. Roll out the remaining marzipan and cut into strips about ¼″ (5mm) wide and long enough to fit between the two strips at the top and bottom of the cake. Spread them with apricot jam and fix in place as shown.

5 Measure the circumference of the cake along the top edge. Measure the height of the cake and add on ¾″ (2cm) so that the icing when applied will extend above the top edge of the cake. Brush the middle section of the cake between the upright strips with water to help the icing stick to the sides. Roll out 1lb (450g) fondant icing on a surface dusted with cornflour. Cut out a piece of icing according to the measurements taken. Fix to the sides of the cake, smoothing the icing into the joins between the upright strips. Allow to dry for at least 4 or 5 hours.

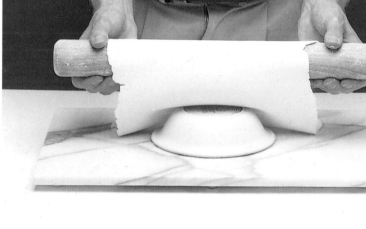

7 Roll out the icing and cut out two shapes for the handles (being cut out in the photograph) and one handle for the lid (on the marble surface; also see p. 21).

6 To make the dustbin lid, roll out 8oz (225g) gelatin icing and lay over an upturned dessert bowl of about 6″ (15cm) in diameter. Trim the icing to the edge of the bowl and allow to dry overnight. Gather up the remaining icing and knead together (add a little water if it has dried out).

8 Allow the dustbin handles to dry against a glass as illustrated. Fix to the sides of the dustbin with royal icing.

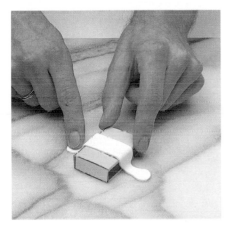

9 Allow the handle for the dustbin lid to dry over a matchbox with the ends of the handle flat against the work surface. Fix to the dustbin lid with a little royal icing.

10 Using food colours, mix up several shades of blue and decorate the cake as illustrated. Paint all over in a light blue and leave to dry. A second coat of colour can be applied as in the photograph with the bristles of the brush splayed out, dabbing the food colour on to the icing to produce a mottled effect for character.

11 Using a darker blue paint one side of each groove of the dustbin to create shadow. Leave to dry.

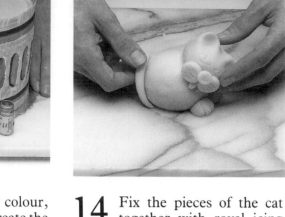

12 Using silver food colour, add highlights to create the illusion of light striking the dustbin.

14 Fix the pieces of the cat together with royal icing and allow to dry for an hour or so before decorating.

13 To make the cat, take the white marzipan and model as illustrated in the photograph. Make the ears by pinching the marzipan and shaping it into triangles. Score the details of the eyes into the marzipan with a cocktail stick, and likewise the details on the paws. The whiskers are made from 1″ (2.5cm) long pieces of modelling wire. If this is not available, cocktail sticks or wooden skewers are just as good. Make sure young visitors do not put them in their mouths.

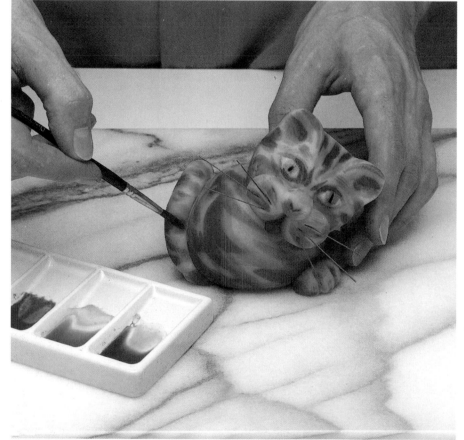

15 Make up a series of yellows and oranges with food colours and paint stripes on the cat. Paint the eyes green and the tongue red. Insert the whiskers into the cheeks.

ASSEMBLY

Place a handful of brightly coloured sweets inside the dustbin and place the lid on top at an angle. Put the cat at the base of the dustbin and scatter a few sweets around it. Put an empty wrapper between its paws.

EASTER CAKE

The traditional simnel cake relies heavily on the use of marzipan and the finished cake is usually browned lightly under the grill for a golden toasted look. These alternative Easter cakes (pictured on p. 29) retain the use of eggs to represent the twelve apostles. The main technique employed here is working in marzipan – one cake features a basketwork design and the other a plait. Neatness is the secret of a professional finish.

Simnel cake is very similar to the rich fruit cake used in the Three-tier Wedding Cake (p. 120), though some recipes leave out the glacé cherries and vary the proportions of dried fruit and candied peel. For these designs we have used the recipe for the top tier (8″/20cm) of the wedding cake. The first illustration shows how a layer of marzipan is baked in the centre of a traditional simnel cake. If you would like to include it, use 8oz (225g) marzipan for the sandwich filling and take extra care when testing to see if the cake has cooked, as a cocktail stick stuck into the marzipan will always come out moist and sticky. The marzipan filling can quite easily be left out, as there is a large amount of marzipan in the decoration of both cakes.

TIMESAVERS

TIMESAVER To simplify the decoration of the eggs, dip them into a solution of food colour and water. Allow the eggs to dry and dip again. Repeated dippings will produce deeper colours. A subtle effect can be achieved by wrapping an egg in the outer skin of an onion. Tie the egg and onion skin in a handkerchief to secure and boil gently for 15 minutes. The egg will be marbled brown and purple, and sometimes green. Allow to cool and rub the eggshell with a little lard for a beautiful sheen.

TIMESAVER Replace the sugared marzipan eggs with chocolate eggs wrapped in coloured foil if you have no time to make them.

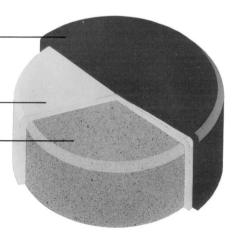

DECORATION 4 hrs
By simplifying the decoration of the eggs an hour can be saved, by using existing eggs 1 hr 30 mins can be saved

MARZIPAN 1 hr 30 mins

COOKING 2 hrs 45 mins

INGREDIENTS

**Basket of eggs
Decoration**
10″ (25cm) round cake board
1lb (450g) yellow marzipan
12oz (350g) white marzipan
apricot jam

Equipment
wire coathanger
ribbon
poster paints
flowers
feathers

**Plaited marzipan cake
Decoration**
10″ (25cm) thin round cake
board
1½lb (675g) yellow marzipan
12oz (350g) white marzipan
4oz (125g) sifted icing sugar
1 tablespoon warm water
1 teaspoon orange flower
water
apricot jam
2oz (50g) caster sugar

Equipment
food colour

BASKET OF EGGS

1 Blow the eggs that you are going to use in the cake mixture rather than breaking them, so that you can use the shells in the decoration. Insert a needle into the egg at both ends, being sure to puncture the membrane and pierce right through to the yolk. Do not be afraid to break the shell with the needle – you will find that it chips away in small pieces. The hole should be only the size of a pinhead. Place a bowl beneath the egg and blow steadily into one of the holes. It can take a lot of blowing to begin with, but then the egg should trickle out quite easily. Shake the egg to check that it is empty. If you are not happy at the prospect of blowing the eggs, simply hard-boil them before decorating.

2 Using a sharp knife cut the cake into an oval shape with slightly sloping sides. Spread the sides of the cake with apricot jam.

TIPS

In the traditional simnel cake a layer of marzipan is placed on half the un-cooked mixture, then the remaining mixture is spooned on top.

3 Roll out 12oz (350g) yellow marzipan and 8oz (225g) white marzipan on a work surface dusted with icing sugar. Cut the yellow marzipan into about 5 strips ½" (1cm) wide and long enough to reach half way round the cake. Cut the white marzipan into strips the same width and long enough to stretch from top to bottom of the cake. Lay the yellow marzipan strips next to one another on the work surface and secure the ends by laying a ruler or a light weight over them. Fold back alternate strips of the yellow marzipan and insert a strip of the white marzipan up to the edges of the folded back pieces. Once in place, fold back the yellow strips. Now fold back the second lot of yellow strips and repeat the process. Continue like this until you have 'woven' a piece of marzipan long enough to cover half the side of the cake.

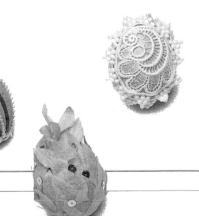

6 As an additional feature (see photograph p. 29), the top of the cake and the handle can be decorated with twisted strips of marzipan. Take the remaining yellow and white marzipan, roll out and cut from each three strips ¾" (2cm) wide. Place a yellow strip on top of a white one and stick them together using egg white or apricot jam. Gently twist each yellow and white strip and decorate the handle as shown. Fix the first end in place by pinching it, wind the strip round then pinch the second end to join the first.

4 Before attaching the marzipan to the cake gently press the top and bottom edges and each end of the woven piece with the ruler so that the individual strips are squeezed together. Do not press so hard as to cut through the pieces, just aim to 'weld' them together. Stick the marzipan to the cake with apricot jam – another pair of hands could come in useful here if you are worried about breaking the weave. Repeat the entire process and marzipan the second half of the cake. Make sure that the seams are at the ends of the cake so that they can be covered with ribbon bows.

7 As the eggs are not to be eaten they can be decorated in any number of ways. In this instance poster paints are used to create bold and colourful designs.

TIPS

Tie two bows of yellow or gold ribbon and attach at the base of the handle so that the bows cover the seam of the woven marzipan. When the paint on the eggs has dried, pile them on top of the cake and fill in any gaps with flower heads, ribbon bows or feathers.

5 To make the basket handle, take a piece of wire – a wire coathanger is ideal. Fold it into a gentle curve and wrap in yellow or gold ribbon. Cover each end of the handle with a small piece of cling film and insert into the cake.

PLAITED MARZIPAN CAKE

1 Turn the cake upside down and prepare it for decoration as for the Three-tiered Wedding Cake on p. 120. Using a piece of string or cotton, measure the circumference of the cake and note down the measurement. Take 1lb (450g) of the yellow marzipan, roll it out on a work surface lightly dusted with icing sugar and cut three strips ¾" (2cm) wide. To determine the length of the strips, add 3" (7.5cm) to the measurement of the circumference. This additional length will be taken up in the plaiting. Lay the three strips on the work surface and pinch the ends together to secure. To plait the marzipan, take the piece on the right and lay it over the piece in the centre. Take the piece on the left and lay it over the piece now in the centre. Continue right over centre, left over centre, until all the marzipan is plaited. Spread a little apricot jam around the sides of the cake. Fix the plait to the cake.

TIPS

If you want to cut down on the marzipan weaving, cut fewer strips of marzipan and make them wider. Bigger strips are easier to handle, but the result will of course look less intricate.

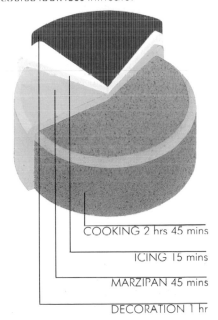

COOKING 2 hrs 45 mins

ICING 15 mins

MARZIPAN 45 mins

DECORATION 1 hr

2 Take the remaining 8oz (225g) yellow marzipan and repeat step 1 to make a plait long enough to go round the top inside edge of the cake. Attach to the cake with a little apricot jam.

6 Take the caster sugar and put in a screw-topped jar with one or two drops of food colour. Screw on the top and shake vigorously to colour the sugar. Paint the eggs with a little egg white, then roll in the coloured sugar. Place on greaseproof paper and allow to dry. Speckled eggs can be made with two or more different colours of sugar.

An alternative way of decorating the eggs (as in the photograph on p. 26) is to paint them red and allow to dry. Dip a paintbrush or old toothbrush in silver food colour and flick spots of colour on to the eggs to produce speckles.

3 To fill the top of the cake with glacé icing, take the sifted sugar and add the warm water. Mix together gently and avoid getting air bubbles in the mixture if possible. Mix in the orange flower water, or an extra teaspoon ordinary water if orange flower water is not available. Carefully pour the icing into the centre of the cake.

4 Allow the icing to spread to the edges of the plaited circle. If any air bubbles should appear in the icing, pop them with a needle and withdraw the needle carefully.

5 To make the eggs, take the white marzipan and divide into 12 equal pieces. Roll each piece into the shape of an egg, each egg to represent an apostle, as is the tradition.

TIPS

As an alternative to rolling the marzipan eggs in coloured sugar, you could knead food colours into the marzipan to produce several pastel shades.

ASSEMBLY

Place the eggs at regular intervals around the plaited top.

PARCEL PATISSERIE

*This cake (shown on p. 33) is made with two 12"
(30cm) square sponge cakes. It is relatively easy to model
as it requires very little cutting. A variety of techniques is
employed in the decoration, from which you can choose
according to the time available and your degree of
confidence. The neat little parcels are individually
wrapped in marzipan and icing – some feature a
marbled finish achieved by incompletely kneading food
colour into the icing. The finishing touches are added
with an icing gift tag and ribbons.*

To make the cake. Cream together the butter or margarine and
sugar until light and fluffy. Add the eggs two at a time and mix
well, followed by a tablespoon of flour. Sift the remaining flours
together and fold into the mixture, followed by the lemon juice.
Grease a 12" (30cm) square cake tin and line with greaseproof
paper. Spoon the mixture into the prepared tin and level off the
surface. Cook in a preheated oven at 160°C/325°F/Gas mark 3 for
1 hour 15 minutes. The cake is ready when risen and firm to the
touch. Cool in the tin for 5 minutes. Turn out of the tin and allow
to cool completely. Remove the lining paper.
  For the filling, soften the cheese, using a little milk if necessary.
Add icing sugar to taste.

This cake (shown on p. 33)

INGREDIENTS

(for one cake)
15oz (425g) butter or margarine
15oz (425g) caster sugar
8 eggs
15oz (425g) self-raising flour
8oz (225g) plain flour
3 tablespoons lemon juice

Filling
12oz (350g) curd cheese
icing sugar
15oz (425g) mandarin orange
segments

Decoration
16" (40cm) square cake board
1½lb (675g) marzipan
1lb (450g) fondant icing
apricot jam

Equipment
food colour
ribbon of various colours
silk flowers if required

TIMESAVERS

TIMESAVER It takes time to plan and
paint the sophisticated peach and silver
stripes on the carrier bag – a simpler
and bolder effect can be achieved by
sponge-printing colours on to the icing.
A cut potato shape can also produce
interesting results.

TIMESAVER In place of the cake
parcels you could put real gifts in the
mouth of the carrier bag.

TIMESAVER Instead of painting the
label on to the bag, make one from
gelatin icing and allow to dry for four
hours. The name can be marked out in
sweets or fake jewels instead of hand-
painted.

DECORATION 2 hrs
1 hour can be saved by
simplifying the decoration

ICING 1 hr 20 mins + drying time

MARZIPAN 1 hr + 6 hrs drying time

COOKING 1 hr 15 mins per cake

1 Cut the two square cakes into oblongs measuring 12″ × 9″ (30 × 23cm). Keep the cut-off pieces. Spread the sweetened curd cheese on one of the cakes. Drain the mandarin oranges in a sieve and press the fruit gently to extract all excess juice. Too much juice can soften the marzipan and seep through to the icing. Place the second cake on top and press gently so that the filling is consolidated.

2 Using a sharp kitchen knife, cut diagonally through the length of the cake from the back edge to a point just above the filling at the front edge so that you end up with a long wedge shape as shown. Now cut a wedge shape into each of the longer sides of the cake as illustrated to give the effect of a carrier bag lying flat.

3 Measure the height and width of the cake at the back and along the sloping edge. Spread the surfaces of the cake with apricot jam. Roll out the marzipan and cut pieces to the dimensions noted. Fix them to the back, sides and top of the cake. Allow to dry for 5 or 6 hours.

4 Lightly dust a work surface with cornflour and roll out the fondant icing. Cover the cake in one piece and smooth the icing on to all the surfaces, pinching it at the corners to make neat seams. With a sharp knife, trim the icing to the edges of the cake. To trim the corners, use scissors. You should then be able to seal the corners neatly. Moisten the edges with water if necessary and press gently together. Keep any icing trimmings. Allow the icing to dry for several hours.

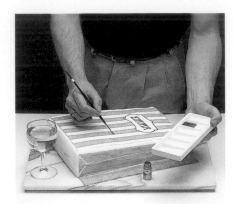

stick or skewer, gently draw over the letters and score the name into the icing. Do not press too hard – even gentle pressure will leave a clear impression. Paint or draw over the indentations using food colour or a food pen.

5 Cut the remaining pieces of cake into shapes to represent parcels spilling out of the mouth of the bag. Spread the parcels with apricot jam and cover with marzipan.

6 To ice the parcels, divide the remaining icing between them and mix in various food colours. It is possible to produce a slightly marbled effect by adding food colour to the icing and kneading only briefly so that the colour is not spread evenly throughout it. Cover the marzipanned parcels and trim the icing neatly at the edges.

7 After the icing on the bag has had a chance to dry, mark out the design for the label on the bag (*see p. 185*), making sure you leave enough space for all the letters in the name. Using greaseproof or tracing paper trace the design. Cut the design out of the paper and place on the cake. Mark it out on the cake with a food colour pen or paintbrush and food colour. Paint stripes on the bag in the colour of your choice. Food colour pens are easier to use than a paintbrush, if you are not particularly handy with one. The stripes and label look good painted in silver. The sides of the cake can be painted a solid colour with silver to emphasize certain details.

8 The name of the recipient can be painted or drawn on the bag using any of the alphabets on *p.185.* Use tracing or greaseproof paper to trace the chosen letters. Place the name in position on the cake. Using a needle, cocktail

9 An additional gift tag can be made from a small amount of gelatin icing. A simple heart shape is pretty, but a square or oblong is just as effective. With an icing cutter or a sharp knife cut a hole and tie a piece of ribbon through it. Choosing whichever greeting is appropriate (*see p. 185*), either mark out the greeting on the surface of the icing while it is still soft as in step 8, or if the gift tag is not to be eaten, you could use graphite paper. Gently lay the graphite paper over the tag and place the tracing paper with the greeting on top of it. Write over the words of the greeting. A graphite trace of them will be left on the gift tag. Paint over the trace.

ASSEMBLY

Place the parcels at the mouth of the carrier bag. They can be prettily decorated with ribbons and silk flowers from the haberdashery department of any large store. The ribbons could be made of coloured icing if you want them to be edible, as could the flowers. Finally make handles for the carrier bag from a thin strip of fondant icing. Attach to the top of the cake as shown with a dab of royal icing.

CHAMPAGNE CELEBRATION

Two 8" (20cm) round madeira sponges layered with fruit preserves and sweetened curd cheese form the basis for this special celebration cake, pictured on p. 41. To make the bottle and the champagne bucket, gelatin icing is moulded on to an empty champagne bottle and a flowerpot – a simple technique that produces spectacular results. Carefully dismantled, each piece of the decoration can be safely removed and reassembled as a permanent souvenir of the party.

To make the cake. Cream the butter or margarine and sugar together until light and fluffy. Add the eggs one at a time and beat into the mixture. After each egg is incorporated add a spoonful of flour and mix again. Sift the remaining flours together and fold into the creamed mixture followed by the lemon juice. Turn the mixture into a greased tin lined with greaseproof paper and level off the top. Place in a preheated oven at 160°C/325°F/Gas mark 3 for about 1 hour 25 minutes or until risen and firm to the touch. Turn out on to a wire cooling rack.

For the filling, mix the curd cheese with a little milk or cream to achieve a spreading consistency and sweeten to taste with icing sugar. Split the cakes in half and sandwich together with the sweetened cheese mixture and a layer of fruit preserve.

TIMESAVERS

TIMESAVER Instead of moulding a champagne bottle from icing, you could put a half-bottle of real champagne in the iced bucket. Either cut into the cake to support the bottle or serve it standing upright leaning against the napkin. A chocolate champagne bottle of the right size wrapped in green foil would also fit the bill.

TIMESAVER Soft pink tissue or a cotton napkin could replace the icing napkin, saving time and providing a contrasting texture to the icing.

DECORATION 2 hrs + 12 hrs drying time
An hour can be saved on the decoration by using the two timesavers

ICING 1 hr + drying time

MARZIPAN 30 mins

COOKING 1 hr 25 mins per cake

1 Assemble the cake as illustrated.

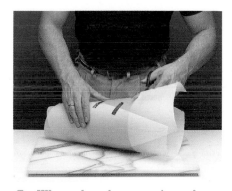

2 Wrap the plant pot in a sheet of greaseproof paper and secure with tape. Trim the paper to the top and bottom edges of the plant pot.

4 Using a sharp knife, cut the cake to the same shape as the pot but slightly smaller than it. The champagne bucket will be exactly the same size as the plant pot – the cake should fit inside it and still leave a ½" (1cm) gap all round. Now roll out 8oz (225g) of marzipan on a work surface lightly dusted with icing sugar and cut out a circle to fit the top of the cake. Spread the top of the cake with the fruit preserve. (It is a good idea to blend it in a liquidizer first.) Place the marzipan on top of the cake. Roll out 1lb (450g) marzipan plus any leftover trimmings. Place the paper pattern on top of the marzipan and cut around it. Spread the sides of the cake with fruit preserve and fix on the marzipan. Leave to dry for a few hours.

3 Using a sharp pair of scissors or a knife cut a straight line through the paper from the top to the bottom edge. Open out the paper. The pattern you have made will act as a guide for marzipanning and icing the cake.

5 Trim off any excess marzipan.

6 Roll out 1lb (450g) of gelatin or tragacanth icing. Lay the paper pattern on top of it and cut around the edge. Save any trimmings and wrap tightly in cling film.

8 Using sticky tape, secure the paper pattern to help keep the icing in place while it dries. Gently smooth the icing into any detail that there is on the pot. Turn the pot upside down and leave the icing to dry for 12 hours or overnight.

7 Lay the icing piece on top of the paper pattern so that the edges match exactly. Place the plant pot on the icing sheet and wrap round.

9 When the icing is dry, remove the paper pattern. Carefully cut the bucket in half with a sharp knife as shown. After 12 hours the icing may still feel rather soft and pliable. If so, it is safest to wrap it back inside the pattern once cut and allow it to dry out completely.

Icing dries as air circulates around it. Wrapping the icing in paper against the plant pot means that very little air can get to it. Once the bucket has been cut, however, you can place both halves inside the plant pot and allow the air to get to the inside of the pieces.

10 Place the two halves of the bucket around the cake and fix together with a little royal icing gently smoothed along the edges. Leave to dry for an hour or so.

11 Paint the bucket with silver food colour.

12 Take any icing trimmings left from making the bucket and roll out again to a sheet about ¼" (5mm) thick. Using a sharp knife cut out four circles, two of which are 1½" (4cm) in diameter and two of which are ¾" (2cm) in diameter. Cut two circles of icing ¼" (5mm) thick for the handles. Cut out a piece from each handle leaving a ¾" (2cm) gap. Leave the icing pieces to dry completely.

13 Paint the bucket details silver and fix on to the bucket as shown with a little royal icing.

TIPS

Instead of painting the bottle green, which could leave brushstrokes, you could knead green food colour into the icing before laying it over the bottle. You might not end up with the same intensity of green, but you won't have to wait for the paint to dry to continue.

14 To make the champagne bottle, take a real (empty) champagne bottle and dust lightly with a little cornflour. Roll out 8oz (225g) gelatin or tragacanth icing and lay over the bottle so that it covers half of it. Gently smooth the icing to the shape of the bottle.

15 Using a sharp knife, trim the icing while soft so that exactly half the bottle is covered. You will find that most bottles are made in two halves and that the glass has a seam running down it. Try to cut the icing to the seam so that you have two exact halves. Because the bottle will be seen sticking out of the bucket, you will not need an entire bottle, and will need to trim off about a third. Allow the icing to dry over the bottle overnight or for 12 hours. As with the icing bucket, it may be that when you remove the icing from the bottle it will still be pliable. If time permits, allow the icing to sit on the bottle until it is completely hard, or if not, tie several pieces of ribbon around the icing to keep it in shape and let it dry out completely in the air while you make the other half of the bottle.

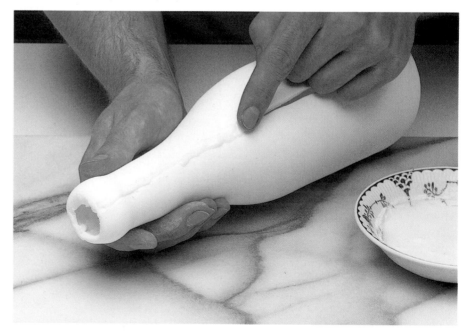

16 Fix the two halves of the bottle together, spreading the seams with a little royal icing. Allow to dry for a couple of hours.

17 Using the label designs and monograms on *p. 183* mark out the bottle with the help of a sheet of graphite paper. Paint the bottle green.

18 Using gold, red and silver food colours, paint on the detail as illustrated.

TIPS

If you decide to colour the icing green you will need to use gold foil for the label and round the neck of the bottle, as gold paint won't take on top of coloured icing. Or you could make a label from gelatin icing and fix it to the bottle with royal icing.

19 Place the bottle inside the bucket, fixing it to the surface of the cake with royal icing.

20 Take the remaining 8oz (225g) gelatin or tragacanth icing and colour it pink. Roll out the icing and cut into oblong shapes for the napkin.

Drape around the bottle and arrange decoratively with at least one or two pieces hanging over the edge of the bucket.

ASSEMBLY

Cut two lengths of ribbon and thread through the bucket handles and all around the cake. Place the cork at the base of the bucket.

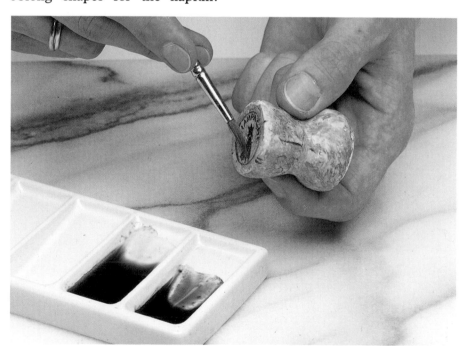

21 Take any remaining icing and shape into a cork. When the icing has dried, stipple it with brown food colour and leave the paint to dry.

CHRISTMAS WREATH

The Christmas Wreath pictured on p.47 is a quick and simple 10" (25cm) round Christmas fruit cake in a time-honoured tradition. The wreath itself can form part of your Christmas decorations both before you serve the cake and after you have eaten it.

TIMESAVERS

TIMESAVER The wreath on top of the cake can become part of your Christmas decorations once the cake has been cut. If you are not intending to eat any of it, then you can save time by omitting the poinsettias and Christmas roses, which are moulded from icing, and using in their place any suitable tree ornaments. Or you could use shop-bought edibles such as chocolate figures wrapped in foil, nuts and dried fruit.

DECORATION 4 hrs including assembly
Timesavers will cut decoration by up to 2 hrs

ICING 1 hr 30 mins + 8 hrs drying time

MARZIPAN 1 hr + 2 hrs drying time

COOKING 3 hrs 45 mins

INGREDIENTS

Decoration
12" (30cm) round cake board
2½lb (1.1kg) marzipan
2lb (900g) white fondant icing
12oz (350g) fondant icing
coloured Christmas red
1¾lb (825g) gelatin icing
apricot jam
royal icing

Equipment
wire for modelling
artificial leaves for the wreath
stiff card
fir cones
food colours
various Christmas decorations
5 tall thin candles

1 Turn the cake upside down. Place a saucer in the middle of the cake and cut round it and right through the cake with a sharp knife to remove the centre. Hold the knife perfectly vertically to make a neat and regular hole. Wrap the cut-out centre for decoration later.

3 On a work surface lightly dusted with cornflour roll out the white fondant icing into a circle about 18″ (46cm) in diameter. Moisten the surface of the cake with a little water on a pastry brush. Lay the icing sheet over the cake and smooth to the outside edge. Using a large flat-bladed knife held against the side of the cake cut off and keep any excess icing. Cut neatly around the top inside edge with a sharp knife and remove the small circle of icing. Roll out the icing remains and cut into a strip according to the measurements previously taken for the inside of the cake. Brush the inside of the cake with a little water and fix on the icing.

2 Take 8oz (225g) marizpan and roll into a long sausage. Press the marzipan into the gap between the cake and the board, as in the wedding cake (see *p.121*). Trim the marzipan to the edge of the cake with a flat-bladed knife and keep any leftovers. Wrap a piece of string round the cake to measure its circumference and measure its height. Roll out 1lb (450g) marzipan into a strip. Cut a piece to the measurements just taken. Cut in half for ease of handling. Spread the outside of the cake with jam and fix the marzipan to it. Gather together all the leftover pieces of marzipan. Measure the circumference of the cutout centre and cut out a piece to fit (the height of the cake has already been noted). Spread the marzipan with apricot jam (it would be too tricky and messy to spread jam on the inside of the cake) and fix the marzipan in position. Roll out 1lb (450g) marzipan. Use the tin in which the cake was baked as a guide and cut out a circle. Place the saucer in the centre of the circle and cut round it. Keep the cut-out circle. Spread the top of the cake with apricot jam and fix the marzipan to it. Allow to dry for two hours.

4 Trace the pattern for the decoration on *p .190* on to greaseproof paper, ensuring that it is long enough to stretch over the cake from the bottom outside to the bottom inside edge. Cut out the pattern.

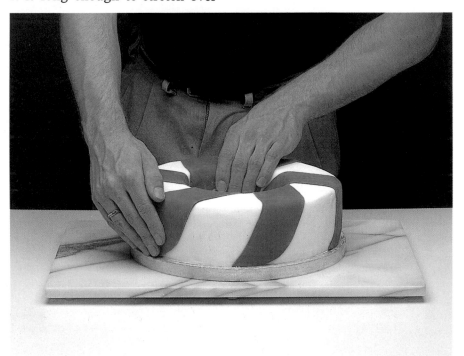

5 On a work surface lightly dusted with cornflour roll out the Christmas red fondant icing. Lay the pattern on the icing and cut around. Place the icing strip over the cake. Dab a little water on the inside of each end of the strip, then smooth down against the sides of the cake. Six of these strips are sufficient to decorate the cake.

6 Take a piece of stiff card. Place the tin in which the cake was baked on the card and draw around it with a pen or pencil. Place the saucer in the centre of the marked-out circle and draw around it. Take a sharp knife or pair of scissors and cut out the circle for the base of the wreath.

7 Assemble the various Christmas decorations that are being used.

10 Paint each petal Christmas red and allow to dry for an hour or so.

8 Take the leaves that form the basis of the wreath and fix to the card circle with tape, staples or glue. Place the first lot decoratively round the outside of the circle, then fill in the inside.

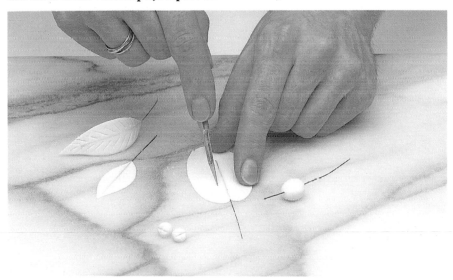

11 When dry, collect the petals together so that you have five larger petals at the base of the flower and five smaller ones on top. Twist the petal wires together to hold the flowers in shape. Make three flowers. Paint the bottom half of the 18 balls green and the top half yellow. Leave to dry for an hour, then paint the crosses red. Fix six balls into the centre of each poinsettia with dabs of royal icing.

9 To make the poinsettia take 4oz (125g) gelatin icing and divide into 10 balls the size of hazelnuts. Cut the modelling wire into 4" (10cm) lengths. Insert a piece of wire into each ball of icing and roll out so the wire extends well into the icing. With a sharp knife cut five of the icing discs into petals 3" (7.5cm) long and the other five into petals 2½" (6.5cm) long. Score veins into the petals with a cocktail stick and allow them to dry over a tin, so that they take on a curved shape, for four hours or until completely dry. Repeat to make enough petals for three poinsettias. Take 4oz (125g) gelatin icing and roll into 18 small balls the size of peas. Cut a small cross into the top of each ball and allow to dry for two hours.

12 To make the Christmas roses cut out a heart-shaped piece of card about 1½″ (4cm) across. For each rose take 4oz (125g) gelatin icing and roll out as thinly as possible. Cut round the card to make five heart-shaped petals. Gently press the edges of the petals between thumb and forefinger to make them as thin as possible, and allow to dry in bun trays, so that they take on a curve, for four hours or until completely dry. Make 15 petals, which will make three roses. Keep any leftover icing.

13 When the petals are dry fix together with small dabs of royal icing to hold the flowers in shape. Allow to rest for at least two hours to give the icing a chance to harden.

SPECIAL FINISHES

To make the centres for the roses cut out 12 2″ (5cm) lengths of yellow cotton. Hold the pieces together and fold in half so that the ends meet in a bunch. Tie together at the bottom with another piece of cotton. Fan out the cotton strands to form a circle. Put a dab of royal icing in the centre of each flower and fix the cotton centres in place. Cut out three ½″ (1cm) circles of icing about as thick as a 10p piece from the trimmings left over. Prick the surface all over with a cocktail stick. Allow to dry for an hour then paint pale yellow. Fix in the middle of the cotton centre with a dab of royal icing. When dry, dust the roses with gold lustre powder. Place a layer of fir cones on the wreath, fixing them in position with royal icing or glue. Fix on the poinsettias and Christmas roses. Fix the remaining decorations on the wreath and allow to rest until the glue or icing has hardened.

Paint the red strips of icing with a thin edging of silver food colour. Paint small dots of silver on the white icing. Allow to dry for about an hour. Place the wreath on top of the cake. Take the five candles and cut to different lengths. Fix the candles in the centre of the cake, securing them to the board with Blu-tak or royal icing.

ASSEMBLY

Be sure not to leave icing the cake until the last moment. It should have plenty of time to dry out completely before you put the wreath on top, or the decoration will stick to the cake and make a mess when you take it off.

GET WELL FRUIT BASKET

A rich farmhouse cake is transformed by the addition of simply modelled marzipan fruit into an imaginative get-well gift. The basket of fruit (see p.53) and the cake board on which it stands could even be wrapped in cellophane secured at the top with a bow. This is a straightforward cake to decorate and its appearance will boost the morale of anyone feeling under the weather.

To make the cake. Sift the flour and spice together and set aside. Cream the butter or margarine with the sugar and treacle until light and fluffy. Beat in the eggs one at a time followed by a tablespoon of flour. Fold in the remaining flour with the fruit and milk and mix thoroughly.

As the cake needs to cook for 2 – 2¼ hours, the tin should be prepared as for a wedding cake. Grease and line the tin with two layers of greaseproof paper. Tie a double layer of brown paper or newspaper round the tin. Spoon the mixture into the tin and level off the top. Cook in a preheated oven at 160°C/325°F/Gas mark 3. To see if the cake is done insert a skewer or cocktail stick into the centre. If no mixture sticks to the skewer, remove the cake from the oven and allow to cool for 5 minutes in the tin. Turn out on to a wire rack and allow to cool.

TIMESAVERS

TIMESAVER Using royal icing to produce a basketweave effect is quite simple after a little practice. However, if you do not want to use an icing bag, you could marzipan the cake in the usual way and then cover it in fondant icing. You could then paint the icing brown to make it look like a basket, or print or stencil the sides of the cake to turn it into a bowl of fruit rather than a basket.

TIMESAVER For a true lover of marzipan this cake is an added inducement to getting well, filled as it is with marzipan fruit. If time does not allow, or the recipient of the cake is not a lover of marzipan, you could fill the basket with real fruit instead.

INGREDIENTS

8oz (225g) self-raising flour
1 teaspoon ground mixed spice
5oz (150g) butter or margarine
5oz (150g) soft brown sugar
1 tablespoon black treacle
2 eggs
4oz (125g) chopped dates
5oz (150g) sultanas
4oz (125g) currants
3 tablespoons milk

Decoration
9″ (23cm) thin round cake board
1lb (450g) yellow marzipan
1¾lb (825g) white marzipan
royal icing made with 1 egg white
4oz (125g) gelatin icing
apricot jam

Equipment
2 × 12″ (30cm) lengths coathanger wire
2 yards (2m) baby ribbon
12″ (30cm) of 1″ (2.5cm) wide ribbon
food colours
lustre powder
edible baker's glaze

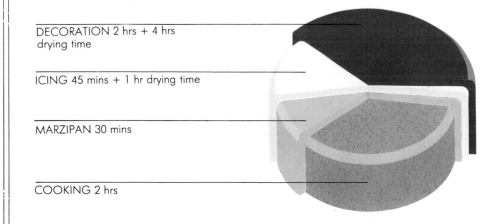

DECORATION 2 hrs + 4 hrs drying time

ICING 45 mins + 1 hr drying time

MARZIPAN 30 mins

COOKING 2 hrs

1 Turn the cake upside down. Using a sharp knife, cut the square on the diagonal into an oval shape. Trim the sides to produce a gently sloping edge.

2 On a work surface lightly dusted with icing sugar roll out 8oz (225g) yellow marzipan. Spread the top of the cake with apricot jam and place it jam-side down on the marzipan. With a sharp knife trim round the edge of the cake and then smooth the marzipan surface, making sure that the edges are neat. Measure the depth of the cake. Wrap a piece of string round the cake to determine its circumference. Roll out 8oz (225g) marzipan and cut out a strip to the measurements just noted. It can be a good idea to cut the piece into two halves to make handling easier. Spread the sides of the cake with apricot jam and fix the marzipan to the sides.

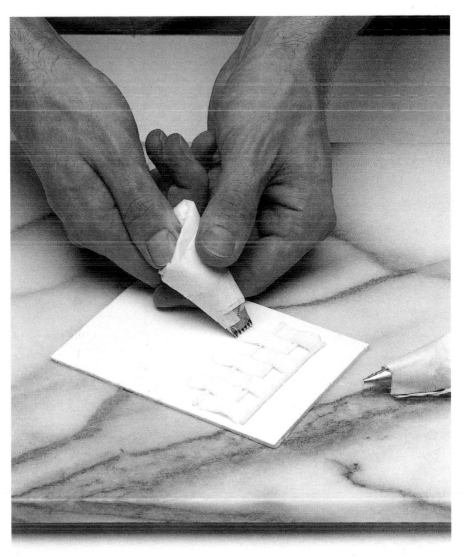

3 This photograph shows the basket weave on a separate piece of icing to make the steps easier to see. The weave is created using icing nozzles Nos 2 and 9. Fix each nozzle to a separate icing bag and fill with 2 tablespoons royal icing. Begin by piping two vertical lines ½" (1cm) apart with nozzle No 2, working from top to bottom of the cake. Take the bag fitted with nozzle No 9 and hold against the top edge of the cake right up to the first vertical line. Pipe a 1" (2.5cm) length of icing stretching over the second vertical line. Pipe a second similar piece of icing leaving a gap the thickness of the icing nozzle between the first and second lengths. Continue in this way to the bottom of the cake leaving gaps between each 1" (2.5cm) piece. Take the bag fitted with nozzle No 2 and pipe a third vertical line joining up the ends of the 1" (2.5cm) pieces just piped. Take the bag fitted with nozzle No 9 and hold against the second vertical line. Begin piping 1" (2.5cm) lengths in the gaps left, stretching over the third vertical line. Take the bag fitted with nozzle No 2 and pipe a fourth vertical line joining up the ends of the 1" (2.5cm) pieces just iced. Continue piping in this way until the whole cake is iced, then leave to dry for one hour.

4 Make up a number of brown food colours and paint the sides of the cake in several shades. Allow to dry for an hour.

5 Dust the side of the cake with edible gold lustre powder.

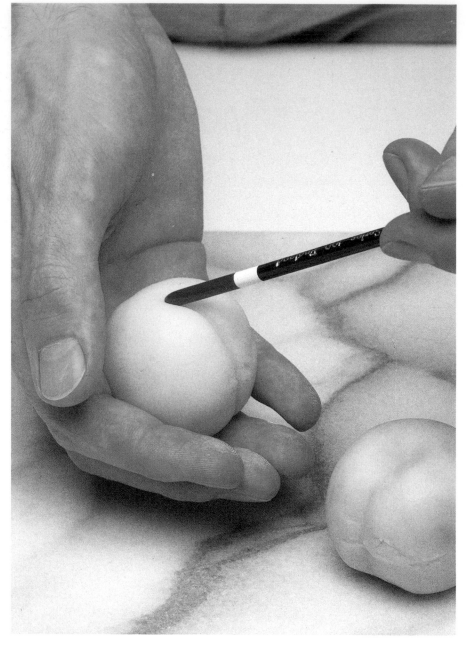

6 A dozen pieces of fruit and grapes are enough for this cake. Each fruit is moulded from about 2oz (50g) white marzipan. For the peaches, oranges and apples, begin by rolling a ball of marzipan. For the oranges and apples, add dimples by pressing the end of a paintbrush into the top and bottom of the ball before allowing it to dry. In the case of the orange, the effect of the skin is created by gently stippling with the end of a fine paintbrush all over the fruit. For the peach gently press the handle of a paintbrush into the side of the fruit to create the characteristic indentation. Make the grapes from smaller slightly elongated marzipan balls. For a banana roll a sausage shape and mould the ends into rounded points. Bend into shape. Flatten the sides slightly as in a real banana. To make a pear, pinch and mould one half of the ball to create the required shape. Add other fruits of your choice. Allow to dry for four hours before proceeding.

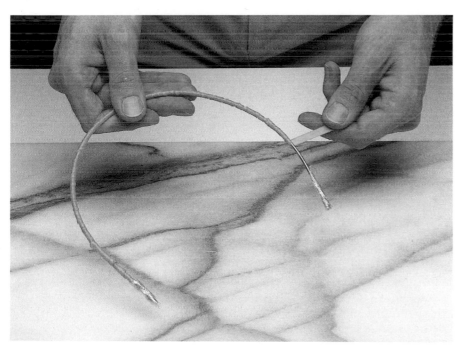

7 To paint the fruit make up a series of shades of food colour relevant to your choice of fruits. In most cases a simple wash of one colour can be brushed on to the fruit and left to dry. However, if you feel adventurous, several shades can be painted on the same fruit. Merge the colours where they meet to produce a delicate bloom. This is done with a moistened brush while the colours are still wet.

8 Take two 12″ (30cm) lengths of coathanger wire and bend into a horseshoe shape. Wrap both wire pieces in lengths of baby ribbon. Wrap the ends of the wire in cling film, as they will be pushed into the cake to the depth of 1″ (2.5cm).

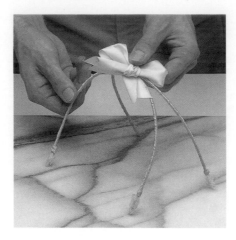

9 Tie the handles in position with a ribbon bow at the top.

10 Gently press the handles into the cake.

11 Take the 4oz (125g) gelatin icing and roll into a sheet on a work surface lightly dusted with cornflour. With a sharp knife cut out 12 spear-shaped leaves about 1½″ (4cm) long. Score veins into the leaves with a cocktail stick. Allow some leaves to dry over a rolling pin and bend others up at the edges to produce a 'v' in cross-section. Leave for four hours to dry. When dry paint green and allow to dry for a further hour. Add a shine to the surface of the leaf with edible baker's glaze.

ASSEMBLY

Pile the fruit on top of the cake. If necessary fix in place with a dab of royal icing. Fill any gaps between the fruit with leaves. Place one or two pieces of fruit on the board for a pleasing effect.

HAND OF CARDS

This striking design (see p.57) is based on blocks of cake bought in a supermarket. We have used four blocks measuring about 6 × 4" (15 × 10cm). The cakes are arranged quite simply and the cards are made from gelatin icing and fanned out on top. You can use the symbols on the cards to convey a message. The King and Queen of Hearts joined by the Ace of Diamonds would be suitable for an engagement party, and a hand of pontoon adding up to 21 would make an unusual 21st birthday cake.

INGREDIENTS

Decoration
12" (30cm) square thin cake board
1lb (450g) marzipan
1lb (450g) fondant icing
12oz (350g) gelatin icing
apricot jam
royal icing

Equipment
food colours
ribbon

TIMESAVERS

TIMESAVER A quicker cake to make on the same theme would be a card table. Cover the cake with green icing to represent baize. When it has dried you could lay out a real hand of cards, say a dummy hand of bridge. Other items such as scoring pads and pencils could be arranged on the cake as part of the gift.

TIMESAVER The cards could be placed in a run instead of fanned out in a hand to avoid the need to cut and shape. Display them slightly overlapping in a straight line. Bear in mind that number cards take less time to paint than royal cards, especially if you are using cutters to make the symbols.

DECORATION 2 hrs 30 mins +
5 hrs drying time
Decoration could be cut to 30
     mins, see Timesavers

ICING 30 mins + 8 hrs drying time

MARZIPAN 45 mins + 2 hrs
drying time

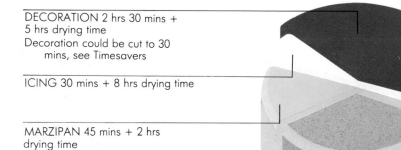

1 Assemble the cakes by placing three side by side lengthways and the fourth cake below the other three as shown. The size of the individual cards is dictated by the size of the cake block. In this instance the assembled cakes allow for cards that are 7" (18cm) long and 4½" (11.5cm) wide. Take your measurements and draw three cards on a piece of greaseproof or tracing paper with each card at an angle to the others, in such a way that the resulting template fits within the block of the cake. Cut out the template.

2 Place the template on the block of cake and cut the cake to its shape.

4 On a work surface lightly dusted with cornflour roll out 1lb (450g) fondant icing. Place the icing over the cake and gently smooth along the edges. Using a flat-bladed knife held against the side of the cake, trim off the excess icing. Allow the icing to dry overnight or for about 8 hours. Now when the cards are placed on the cake they will be easily removable. If the icing is even remotely tacky or sticky to the touch, the cards may stick, which would make cutting difficult.

3 Spread the top of the cake with apricot jam. On a work surface lightly dusted with icing sugar roll out 8oz (225g) marzipan. Place the template on the marzipan and cut around the edge. Fix the marzipan to the surface of the cake. Measure the depth of the cake. Take a piece of string and wrap round the edge of the cake to determine its circumference. Roll out the remaining marzipan and cut a strip to the depth of the cake and the length of the sides. It will be easier and perhaps produce a neater edge if this strip of marzipan is cut in half and applied in two sections. Spread the sides of the cake with jam and fix on the marzipan. Allow to dry for two hours.

5 On a piece of greaseproof or tracing paper mark out the shape of one card. Roll out 12oz (350g) gelatin icing and using the template for the single card, cut out three shapes. Allow to dry for at least 4 hours until completely dry.

6 Take a pack of cards and select the three to be used in the cake. Trace the designs on to greaseproof or tracing paper, increasing the size of each motif if necessary to match the size of your cards. Put a piece of graphite paper over the icing card and lay the tracing on top. Draw over the design to transfer each motif into position on the icing card. Make the three cards in this way and paint with the appropriate food colours. Allow to dry for an hour or so.

8 If you are a little hesitant about painting with food colours, the various symbols for the suits can be cut out of gelatin icing with pastry cutters and fixed on the card with dabs of royal icing. You can buy school rulers from certain shops which feature stencils of letters and numbers. One such could be used, in conjunction with food colour pens, to mark out the letters and numbers on the cards.

7 To assemble the cake place the three cards overlapping on the surface of the cake. Ribbon of various colours, possibly chosen to match those in the cards, can be added to the sides of the cake and fixed in place with royal icing.

HALLOWEEN PUMPKIN

A warm, spicy parkin will keep out the cold on Halloween. This pumpkin (pictured on p. 61) is made of three 9″ (23cm) round cakes piled one on top of the other and features simple carving. Parkin lends itself admirably to this technique as it is moist and dense and therefore easy to cut. The orange fondant icing 'skin' and the candle flame flickering behind the cut-out features complete the illusion.

To make the cake. Grease a 9″ (23cm) round cake tin and line with greaseproof paper. Place the flour and oats in a mixing bowl and sift in the soda, salt and ginger. Place the butter or margarine, treacle, syrup and sugar in a saucepan and heat gently until the fat has melted. Cool slightly and add to the dry ingredients together with the milk. Mix thoroughly. Pour the mixture into the tin and bake in a preheated oven at 180°C/350°F/Gas mark 4 for about 50 minutes, or until firm to the touch. Leave the cake in the tin for 15 minutes, then turn out to cool on a wire tray. Store for several days before eating. Do not be anxious if your parkin appears to sink slightly on cooling. Parkin tends to do this, but as you will see in the step-by-step instructions, the centre of each cake is cut out and not used in the finished pumpkin.

TIMESAVERS

TIMESAVER If you lack either the time or the confidence to hollow out the centre of the pumpkin to take the candle, a whole pumpkin with a candle sitting on the top would be a quicker alternative. You can paint the features in black on the surface of the cake.

TIMESAVER You can ice the cake in one go. Roll out the coloured fondant into a circle large enough to cover the entire cake, and lay it on the cake board, which you have lightly dusted with cornflour. Put the marzipanned cake in the centre of the icing and moisten the marzipan all over to make it sticky. Fold the icing up the sides of the cake without bothering to smooth out the creases. Twist the surplus at the top into a stalk and leave to dry. The stalk can be painted afterwards.

INGREDIENTS

Made with 3 × 9″ (23cm) round parkin cakes.

(for one cake)
8oz (225g) wholemeal flour
8oz (225g) rolled oats
½ teaspoon bicarbonate of soda
½ teaspoon salt
1 teaspoon ground ginger
4oz (125g) butter or margarine
4oz (125g) black treacle
4oz (125g) golden syrup
4oz (125g) soft brown sugar
6 fl oz (175ml) milk

Decoration
12″ (30cm) round cake board
2lb (900g) yellow marzipan for the pumpkin
8oz (225g) white marzipan for the spider
1½lb (675g) fondant icing coloured orange
apricot jam
a little royal icing

Equipment
one or two candles or a nightlight
food colour

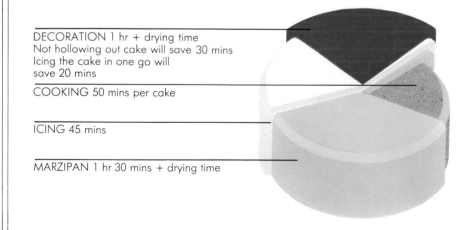

DECORATION 1 hr + drying time
Not hollowing out cake will save 30 mins
Icing the cake in one go will save 20 mins

COOKING 50 mins per cake

ICING 45 mins

MARZIPAN 1 hr 30 mins + drying time

1 Cut the centre out of each cake using a teapot lid as a guide. Keep the centres and enjoy them later with friends and a cup of tea!

3 Pile the cakes one on top of the other.

2 Roll out a small amount of the marzipan and cut out a strip to the depth of the cake. Measure the circumference of the teapot lid to determine the length of the strip.

Brush the marzipan with a little apricot jam and fix on to the cut inside edge of the cake. Repeat with the other two cakes.

This will tell you how wide each of the marzipan segments should be at the top, in the middle and at the bottom, and allow you to take into account the curve of the cake. Roll out the marzipan and, using a sharp knife, cut out 6 segments according to the measurements just calculated. Gently press the edges of the segments to round them off – this will emphasize the segments once applied to the pumpkin. Brush each segment with apricot jam and fix to the side of the cake. Allow to dry for several hours or overnight before proceeding.

4 Using a sharp knife, carve the pile of cakes as illustrated into the beginnings of a pumpkin shape.

5 The pumpkin will be made with 6 individual marzipan segments, so to find out how big each will be, use a piece of cotton or string to measure the height of the cake and its circumference at the widest point. Measure the circumference of the cake again around the opening on the top and around the bottom where the cake meets the board. Note down each of the circumference measurements, then divide each figure by 6.

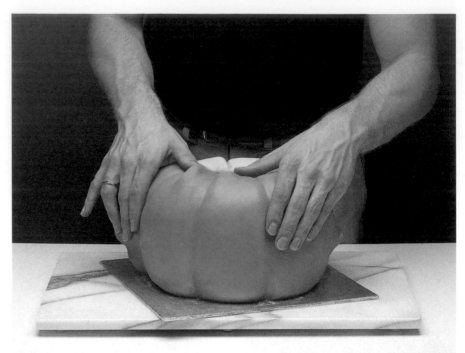

6 Using a food colour pen or a cocktail stick, mark out the eyes, nose and mouth as illustrated.

7 Using a sharp pointed knife, cut the marzipan and cake through to the hollow centre. If unsure, proceed steadily by removing small pieces one at a time. Do not be afraid that the cake will collapse in on the cut-out detail. If the parkin has been stored for a short time it will have a lovely moist density which makes it perfect for carving in this way.

8 Once again measure the height and circumference of the now marzipanned cake. Take half of the orange fondant icing and roll out on a work surface dusted with cornflour. Cut out a piece of icing the same height as the cake and as long as *half* its circumference. Moisten the joins between the marzipan segments with water and gently press the icing on to the cake and into the joins (an extra pair of hands can be very useful at this point). Do not be worried if the icing creases at the top of the cake. It is not important to try and flatten out the creases as they add to the natural look of the pumpkin. Trim any excess icing to the hollowed-out centre. Repeat this process with the other half of the cake. Before the icing dries, gently smooth it over the eyes, nose and mouth so that the edges become clearly outlined. Using your kitchen knife, cut out the icing to expose the eyes, nose and mouth.

9 Take the white marzipan and mould the spider as illustrated. Score the details of the eyes and mouth into the marzipan with a cocktail stick. Allow to dry for several hours before fixing together with a little royal icing. Paint the spider in the colour of your choice, using either food colours and a paintbrush or edible food colour pens.

ASSEMBLY

Secure the candle(s) or nightlight in the centre of the cake. Fix the spider at an angle on top of the cake with royal icing. Light the candles, turn out the lights and Happy Halloween!

BOX OF ROSES

Red roses on St Valentine's Day are the traditional expression of love. Here the romantic theme is presented in a chocolate cake ingeniously concealed in an attractively decorated icing box (see p. 67). The long-stemmed scarlet roses too are moulded from gelatin icing.

To make the cake. First make Mixture 1. Mix the cocoa and sugar in a pan, then beat in the eggs and add the milk. Cook gently, being careful to stir all the time, until the mixture has thickened and starts to bubble gently. Remove the pan from the heat and allow to cool slightly.

For Mixture 2, cream the butter and sugar together until fluffy. Add the eggs and beat vigorously. Sift the flour and baking powder and fold into the mixture, alternating with the milk until combined. Combine mixtures 1 and 2. Grease and line a 12″ (30cm) square tin. Pour the mixture into the tin and level off the top. Bake in a preheated oven at 180°C/350°F/Gas mark 4 for about 1 hour 10 minutes. The cake is cooked if it is firm to the touch. Leave in the tin for 5–10 minutes before turning on to a wire rack to cool.

For the filling, break the chocolate into pieces and place in a bowl over a pan of boiling water. When melted, remove the bowl and allow the chocolate to cool. Bring the cream to the boil and add a few drops of vanilla flavouring. Remove the cream from the heat and gradually beat in the melted chocolate. Leave the mixture to cool, then beat again thoroughly. The mixture will almost double in volume and become paler. This process takes a great deal of effort if you are using a hand whisk and is better done in an electric mixer. If you do not have an electric mixer, whisk until the mixture stiffens. If you grow tired before the ganache is of spreading consistency, add a little sifted icing sugar and fold in. Ganache hardens quite soon after it has been whisked, so use immediately.

INGREDIENTS

Cake: Mixture 1
7oz (200g) cocoa powder
12oz (350g) soft brown sugar
2 large eggs (size 1 or 2)
9 fl oz (250ml) milk

Mixture 2
8oz (225g) butter
12oz (350g) soft brown sugar
4 large eggs (size 1 or 2)
1lb (450g) plain flour
6 teaspoons baking powder
9 fl oz (250ml) milk

Ganache filling
13oz (375g) plain chocolate
9 fl oz (250ml) double cream
a few drops of vanilla flavouring

Decoration
14″ (35cm) square cake board
1lb (450g) fondant icing
1¼lb (565g) marzipan
1½lb (675g) gelatin icing for the box, rose leaves and gift tag
1lb (450g) gelatin or tragacanth icing for the roses
apricot jam
a little royal icing

Equipment
food colour
skewers
modelling wire
white tissue paper
cellophane

TIMESAVERS

TIMESAVER Making the roses takes practice. If you don't have the time to acquire it, a dozen real red roses inside the icing box would make a perfect gift.
TIMESAVER You could leave the box plain white and tie a wide red silk ribbon round it to make a generous bow at the side. Or you could knead red and pink food colours into the icing, mixing them incompletely to create a marbled effect when rolled out.

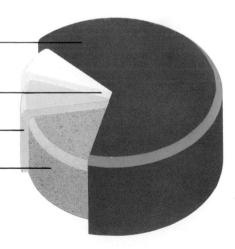

DECORATION 4 hrs
By using real roses 1 hr 30 mins can be saved
Simplifying box saves 30 mins

ICING 25 mins + drying time

MARZIPAN 25 mins + drying time

COOKING 1 hr 10 mins

Cut the cake into two 12″ × 6″ (30 × 15cm) rectangles. If flavouring the cake with liqueur, sprinkle the cut surface of both cakes and allow to soak in. Spread the top of one cake with chocolate ganache and sandwich the cakes together.

1 Spread the top and sides of the cake with apricot jam. Roll out the marzipan into a large sheet. Measure the top and sides of the cake and cut out pieces of marzipan to these dimensions. Cover the top and sides of the cake with marzipan. Allow to dry for several hours.

2 Dust a work surface with cornflour and roll out the fondant icing into a sheet large enough to cover the whole cake. Lay the icing over the cake and smooth over the top and sides. Pinch the icing at the corners to make neat seams. Use scissors to cut the corners and a sharp knife to trim the icing along the edges. Leave the icing to dry for several hours.

3 Roll out the gelatin icing and cut out four pieces to make the box. The sides of the box should be 1½″ (4cm) higher than the iced cake and ½″ (1cm) longer than the length and width of the cake respectively, so that they will fit neatly over it (see step15) without touching. Let the pieces for the box dry on a flat surface until rigid, turning them over after 4 or 5 hours so that both surfaces come into contact with the air.

4 Using a ruler and a food colour pen, mark the sides of the box to indicate where the stripes should be drawn.

5 Draw the stripes on the box.

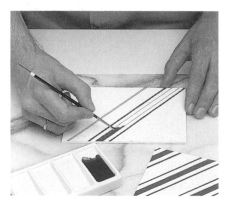

6 Fill in the colour with a paint-brush or food colour pen.

7 Spread the edges of the box pieces with royal icing and press together carefully to make the box. Remove any icing that may squeeze out at the seams with a sharp knife. Once the box is assembled, allow to dry.

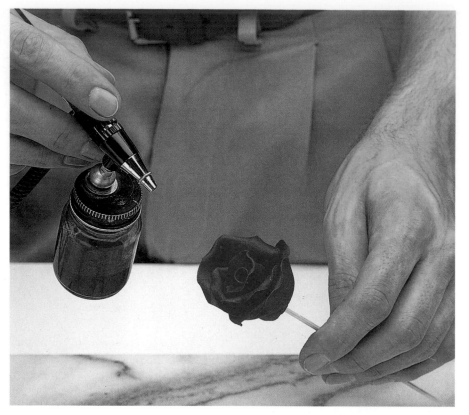

8 The technique of making roses is fully described in the Three-tier Wedding Cake (see p. 125). use the same technique, but make the roses on skewers. A good idea is to secure the skewer in a block of florist's oasis – this will allow you to use both hands to make and shape the rose. A deep red rose is the traditional gift for Valentine's Day, but it is worth noting that it is rather difficult to achieve the depth of colour required by simply adding red to icing. In order to produce a truly deep red it would be necessary to add so much food colour that the texture of the icing would become unmanageable. Another way of achieving a good red is to add a certain amount of red to the icing and then complete the colouring by brushing red on to the dried rose or, as in the photograph, spraying colour on to the flower with an airbrush.

9 To make the rose leaves take a piece of gelatin icing the size of a hazelnut and insert a 3″ (7.5cm) piece of wire through it. Roll out the icing so that the wire runs through its centre. Using a sharp knife, cut out a petal shape, leaving about 1½″ (4cm) wire sticking out of the leaf. Allow the leaf to dry over a rolling pin so that it takes on a gentle curve. Rose petal shapes are available in some shops, and these can be used for cutting round. They also have details of leaf veins, which can be pressed into the soft icing for added authenticity.

10 Once the leaves have dried, paint them green.

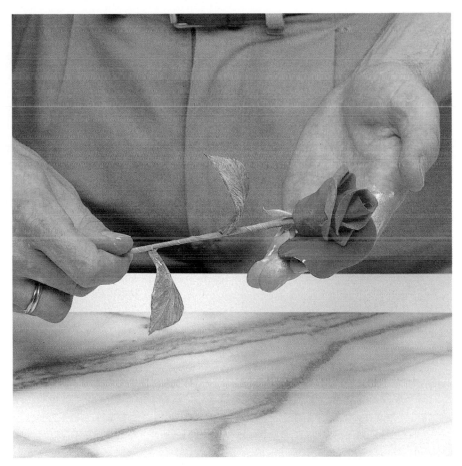

11 To prepare the stem of the rose, cut four 1½″ (4cm) pieces of gutteroll into long slim spear shapes to form the calyx. Gather the four pieces and hold them at the top of the skewer. Secure them to the skewer by wrapping gutteroll around the bottom ½″ (1cm) of the strips. Continue wrapping the skewer for about 2″ (5cm). Take a dried rose leaf and hold the extending wire against the skewer. Continue wrapping the gutteroll over the wire so that the leaf is attached to the skewer. Place another leaf further down the skewer and continue with the gutteroll until the skewer is covered. Bend back the strips of gutteroll at the top of the skewer to form the calyx. This will leave about 1″ (2.5cm) of skewer uncovered.

12 The flower head can be made on the prepared skewer. Here the last petal is being wrapped around the stem.

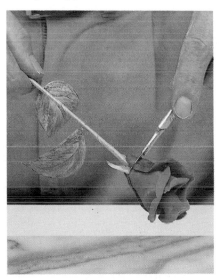

13 Trim the petal level with the calyx using a scalpel or a very sharp knife.

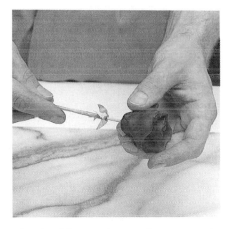

14 Alternatively, flower heads can be made separately and fixed to the skewers once they have dried.

To make an authentic bouquet of roses, at least some of the flowers should be buds, or barely open blooms.

ASSEMBLY

15 Place over the cake.

Place the roses in the box and gently drape red ribbon tied in a bow over the roses and box.

A gift tag can be added as in the main photograph.

16 Place one or two sheets of cellophane and white tissue paper in the box. Do not press down on the cake more than necessary. Make sure the icing has had time to dry sufficiently, or the paper may stick to it.

TIPS

This box has been very carefully decorated so that all the stripes match up – the result is smart and professional. A less time-consuming finish can be achieved by printing heart patterns on the box with a sponge or a potato cut to shape.

BIRTHDAY BREAKFAST

Three 12" (30cm) square moist apple cinnamon cakes are transformed by clever sugarwork into a celebration birthday breakfast table. The cake, pictured on p. 73, illustrates the versatility of icing as a modelling medium. The crockery and cutlery is simply moulded by laying gelatin icing over a real table setting. The authentic-looking multi-petalled carnations, on the other hand, may require a little practice to perfect. Delicate brushwork completes the gift and the decorations can be kept as a souvenir of a lovely day.

To make the cake. Grease a 12" (30cm) square cake tin and line with greaseproof paper. Sift the flour and cinnamon into a bowl and stir in the sugar and raisins. Mix in the melted butter or margarine along with the eggs, milk and apple. Beat until smooth. Transfer the mixture to the tin and bake in a preheated oven at 180°C/350°F/Gas mark 4 for 45–50 minutes. The cake is ready when it springs back when lightly pressed. Remove the cake from the tin and allow to cool on a wire rack, make three.

For the filling, soften the curd cheese and add icing sugar to taste. Stir in the calvados to taste, without making the mixture too runny.

TIMESAVERS

TIMESAVER If you prefer, use a real cup and saucer, carnation, croissant, birthday card etc. on top of the cake instead of making them from icing.

TIMESAVER We have made a very large cake in order to accomodate all the iced novelties on top. It will serve a sizeable gathering. If you wanted to make a smaller cake, you could change the decoration on top to suit. Mould a large dinner plate and make an icing breakfast of bacon, eggs and mushrooms, or the recipient's favourite meal.

INGREDIENTS
(for one cake)
10oz (300g) self-raising flour
1½ teaspoons ground cinnamon
8oz (225g) soft brown sugar
4oz (125g) raisins
4oz (125g) butter or margarine, melted
2 large eggs, beaten
6 fl oz (175ml) milk
8oz (225g) dessert apples, peeled, cored and chopped

Filling
1½lb (675g) curd cheese
icing sugar to taste
calvados to taste

Decoration
16" (40cm) square cake board
2lb (900g) fondant icing coloured blue for the tablecloth
1lb (450g) fondant icing left white for the overcloth
2lb (900g) marzipan for the cake
12oz (350g) marzipan for the croissant and butter rolls
1¾lb (800g) gelatin icing for the crockery, spoon and vase
1lb (450g) tragacanth or gelatin icing for the carnations
apricot jam
baker's glaze
royal icing

Equipment
food colour
gutteroll
wooden skewers
decorative cutters

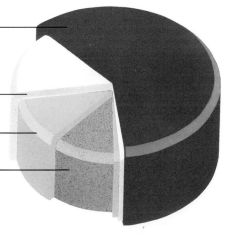

DECORATION 4 hrs + 12 hrs drying time
By cutting down on the crockery up to 2 hrs saved on decoration.
By making a smaller cake up to 2 hrs 30 mins can be saved.

ICING 1 hr + drying time

MARZIPAN 45 mins

COOKING 45 mins per cake

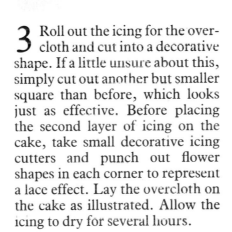

1 Spread the cakes with the filling and sandwich on top of each other. Spread the top of the cake with apricot jam. Roll out half the marzipan. Using the tin in which the cakes were baked as a guide, cut out a square of marzi-pan and place on top of the cake. Measure the length and height of the sides of the cake. Roll out the remaining marzipan and cut 4 pieces to the sizes just noted. Spread the pieces with apricot jam and fix to the sides of the cake.

2 On a work surface well dusted with cornflour, roll out the fondant icing for the tablecloth into a large enough square to drape over the cake. Place over the cake and arrange the decorative folds at the corners and sides. Trim off any excess icing.

3 Roll out the icing for the over-cloth and cut into a decorative shape. If a little unsure about this, simply cut out another but smaller square than before, which looks just as effective. Before placing the second layer of icing on the cake, take small decorative icing cutters and punch out flower shapes in each corner to represent a lace effect. Lay the overcloth on the cake as illustrated. Allow the icing to dry for several hours.

4 Using colours of your choice, decorate the tablecloth with a bold check. If you like, using a contrasting colour, paint deli-cate brush strokes to emphasize the lace effect and to indicate the stitching around the edge of the cloth.

5 A homely touch – a slightly lighter blue gives the effect of a woven check.

TIPS

Painting the checks on the tablecloth is quite time-consuming. Instead you could print a check design using two or more 1" (2.5cm) squares cut from a washing-up sponge, with one colour on each. The effect will be 'hand-woven' rather than crisp.

6 Take 6oz (175g) gelatin icing and roll out into a circle. Gently ease the icing into a tea cup, pressing gently against the sides and bottom of the cup to smooth out any creases that might form. Trim the excess icing to the top of the cup. Save any leftover icing. Remember that to reconstitute leftover gelatin icing you should simply add a very little water and knead briefly. Let the icing cup dry overnight.

8 Take 12oz (350g) gelatin icing. Roll out and cover a tea plate and saucer. Gently smooth the icing around the lip of the plate and into the saucer and trim away any excess icing. Leave to dry overnight.

9 Remove the icing crockery from the plate and saucer. Fix the handle to the cup with a little royal icing.

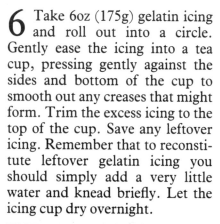

7 Remove the icing cup and using 2oz (50g) gelatin icing roll out a small circle. Take a sharp knife and cut out a handle similar to the one on your teacup. Allow to dry overnight.

10 To make the vase, take a straight-sided drinking glass and measure the height and circumference. Roll out the remaining gelatin icing and cut out a rectangle to the dimension noted. Wrap the icing around the glass. Secure the icing while it dries by wrapping glass and icing in a sheet of greaseproof paper and securing with sticky tape. Let the icing dry overnight.

11 Once dry, remove the glass and secure the join of the vase by spreading with a little royal icing and pressing gently together. To keep the join closed, wrap the vase in paper again and tape up if necessary.

12 Using colours of your choice, decorate the crockery and vase. For this stage of the operation remember that food colour pens could be very useful.

13 To make the croissant, roll out 8oz (225g) of the marzipan on a surface lightly dusted with icing sugar. Cut out a stylized triangle with somewhat extended points, as in the photograph.

14 Roll up the croissant beginning with the base of the triangle facing you. Complete the croissant by folding the remaining point over. Bend the edges of the croissant round to produce the characteristic shape.

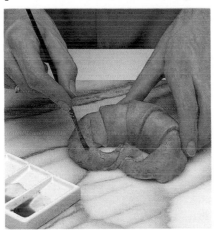

15 Mix up a number of orange, yellow and brown food colours and paint the croissant. Allow to dry and paint over with edible confectioner's or baker's glaze. Use egg white if this is not available.

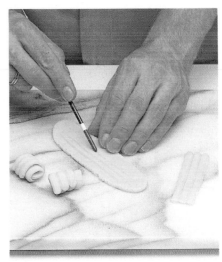

16 To make the butter roll take 4oz (125g) marzipan and roll out. Cut out three 1" (2.5cm) wide strips. Using the end of a paint brush or skewer, deeply score the marzipan with parallel lines. Turn the strips over and roll up so that the scored lines are on the outside. Leave to dry.

17 To make the carnations, roll out the tragacanth (or gelatin) icing as thinly as possible. With a pastry cutter, cut out a circle of icing. Take a sharp knife and make ¼″ (5mm) cuts into the edge of the icing circle at ½″ (1cm) intervals.

18 Using the end of a paint brush or skewer, press on to the surface of the icing and roll backwards and forwards to produce a ruffled effect. Moisten the centre of the icing up to the ruffle.

ASSEMBLY

Place all the separate elements on the cake as illustrated. To ensure that the carnations are secure, it is perhaps a good idea to gently push the ends of the taped skewers into the surface of the cake.

19 Insert a bamboo skewer through the icing into the centre of the flower. Fold the icing circle in half with the point of the skewer inside it. With the skewer lying flat on a work surface fold up one side of the half circle to the centre as illustrated and secure by moistening the icing. Turn the skewer over and repeat so that the half circle has now been folded into an 'S' shape. The flower should dry upside down. To allow it to do this, simply moisten a small piece of icing and stick it to a wall unit above your work surface. Insert the skewer through the icing so that the flower is hanging down below the unit. It is not essential for each stage to be completely dry before continuing. Each flower is made of 4 or 5 iced circles, depending on the fullness of flower required. To add the second layer, moisten the next ruffled circle and thread it on to the skewer allowing it to rest over the shaped centre, then return to the wall unit to dry. When making the flowers it is easier to make all the centres, then all the second layers etc., rather than making one complete flower before going on to the next. This way the various layers have a chance to dry a little before the next layer is applied. Leave the completed flowers to dry overnight.

To make a calyx for the carnation (if such authenticity is required), take a small amount of icing and colour it pale green. Shape it into a rounded pyramid. Using a sharp knife, make five small cuts at intervals around the bottom edge of the mound. Moisten the flat end with a little water and thread on to the skewer, pressing the calyx against the base of the flower to secure it. Leave to dry. Wrap the skewer in gutteroll as with the roses in the Valentine's Day cake.

Additional decorative features in the shape of a birthday card and a folded newspaper can also be made quite easily. To make the newspaper, take 12oz (350g) of gelatin icing and roll out to a rectangle measuring 12″ × 9″ (30 × 23cm). Fold into 3 and allow to dry. To write a newspaper headline, trace letters or words from a real newspaper on to greaseproof paper. Put a piece of graphite paper on the icing newspaper and lay the tracing over the top. Copy over the tracing and then with black food colour or a colour pen paint over the graphite trace.

To make the card, take 8oz (225g) of gelatin icing and roll out thinly. Cut out 2 rectangles measuring 6″ × 4″ (15 × 10cm). Cut corresponding holes in each rectangle with a small icing cutter, then allow to dry. Tie the pieces together with thin ribbon and make small decorative bows. Decorate the front of the card with a design of your choice. You can sign a greeting inside the card in edible food colour pen, then the card can be kept as a reminder of the celebration.

TREASURE ISLAND

Three 9" (23cm) shop-bought chocolate sponge layers are sandwiched together with cream filling to make the island and the gelatin icing treasure chest contains gifts for all the guests at the party. The finished cake with its marzipan palm tree and brightly painted icing shells (see p.79) will make a spectacular centrepiece for any children's party.

To make the filling. Cream the butter or margarine with the icing sugar and add vanilla flavouring to taste.

INGREDIENTS

Filling
6oz (175g) butter or margarine
1lb (450g) icing sugar
vanilla flavouring

Decoration
12" (30cm) round cake board
1½lb (675g) marzipan
1½lb (675g) fondant icing
2½lb (1.1kg) gelatin icing
royal icing
apricot jam

Equipment
small gifts
gold chocolate money
food colours
junk jewellery
lustre powder
½" (1cm) ribbon of various
colours
shells

TIMESAVERS

TIMESAVER The treasure chest and its contents are bound to be the main point of interest for the person receiving the cake. Save time on the other decorations by placing real shells on the sand instead of moulding them from icing.

TIMESAVER Instead of making the decorative corner pieces for the chest, you could encrust it with fake jewels and sequins arranged in formation. Go to the haberdashery department of any major store for inspiration.

DECORATION 2 hrs 30 mins + 2 hrs drying time for the food colour and a total of 12 hrs drying time for the icing

ICING 25 mins + 2 hrs drying time

MARZIPAN 25 mins

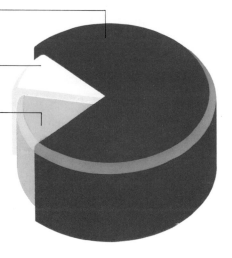

1 Spread the vanilla cream filling between the layers of cake and pile on top of one another.

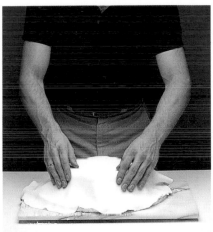

2 Using a sharp kitchen knife trim off the top edge all round the cake and roughly trim the sides to produce an irregular sloping edge. The treasure chest will measure 6 × 3 × 2½″ (15 × 7.5 × 6.5cm), so when you are trimming the cake make sure you still have enough room on top for the chest.

4 On a work surface lightly dusted with cornflour roll out the fondant icing into a sheet large enough to cover the cake and board. Lay the icing over the cake and trim to the edge of the board. Let the icing dry for two hours.

TIPS

Instead of eating the cut-off pieces of cake, chop them roughly and place around the cake before you apply the marzipan. When the cake is iced, you can then paint them to suggest a rocky coastline.

3 Spread the top and sides of the cake with apricot jam. On a work surface lightly dusted with icing sugar roll out the marzipan into a sheet large enough to cover the cake and the board. Lay it over the cake and gently smooth down. It is not necessary to allow the marzipan to dry before proceeding.

5 Make up yellow and pale blue food colours. With a large paintbrush paint a wash of yellow over the island leaving an irregular strip around the edge of the board. Paint this with a wash of pale blue. Put some more yellow on the brush, pressing the bristles into the colour to splay them out. Gently dab at the surface of the wet yellow wash to produce a stippled effect. Repeat on the blue strip with the brush dipped in blue food colour. Let the colours dry for at least two hours.

6 On a work surface lightly dusted with cornflour roll out 12oz (350g) gelatin icing and cut out the following shapes: three rectangles measuring 6 × 2½″ (15 × 6.5cm), two rectangles measuring 2½ × 3″ (6.5 × 7.5cm), two narrow strips measuring 6 × ½″ (15 × 1cm) and two measuring 3 × ½″ (7.5 × 1cm). Allow to dry for at least four hours, turning the pieces over at least once to let the air get to both sides. The body of the chest is made by fixing together two of the large rectangles and the two small rectangles into a box shape as illustrated. Fix in place with royal icing, which for this purpose should be quite stiff. The lid is made with the remaining pieces arranged as shown. When fixed together with royal icing, allow the body and lid of the chest to dry overnight.

and one much darker. When the chest and lid are quite dry, brush them all over with the light brown and allow to dry for an hour. Take the paintbrush and dip into the dark brown, pressing the bristles to splay them out. Brush over the pale brown leaving a trace of separate thin dark lines, as in wood grain. To make a knot hole, bend the painted lines above and below the knot, then fill in with a series of circular brush strokes. This adds visual interest. However, the wood grain effect is interesting without the knot holes if you prefer to leave them out.

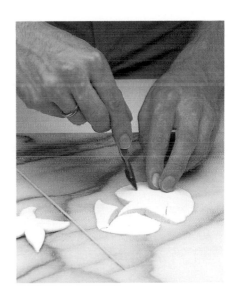

7 Make up two shades of brown food colour, one quite pale

9 To make a starfish roll out 4oz (125g) gelatin icing into a rough circle about 2½″ (6.5cm) in diameter. Trace the starfish shape from the design on *p.189*. Cut out and place the template on the iced circle. Cut round it. Gently press down the edges of the starfish to round them off. With the point of a cocktail stick prick two lines of decorative dots into the icing all around the edge of the starfish. Allow to dry in position on the edge of the cake for at least four hours so that the starfish takes on the curve of the cake before you paint it. To decorate the starfish, brush over with a bright food colour of your choice and leave to dry for an hour.

8 On a work surface lightly dusted with cornflour roll out 8oz (225g) gelatin icing into a large sheet. Using the illustration on *p189* trace out the various designs for the chest trimmings on to greaseproof or tracing paper and cut out. Using the paper templates cut out 20 of the small roughly triangular shapes to be fixed to the corners of the sides and lid of the chest. Also cut out one each of the large and small decorative shapes.

Allow to dry for at least four hours. When dry paint with a number of food colours, or in silver or gold or embellish richly with fake jewels or sequins. Paint a keyhole on the smaller decorative shape if you like. Allow to dry, then fix the large design in the centre of the lid with royal icing and the small one on the front of the chest. Fix the corner pieces at the corners.

10 To make the shells roll out a further 4oz (125g) gelatin icing. You may want to colour the icing first, or perhaps to give a marbled effect by adding two or more colours and incompletely kneading them in so that swirling patterns are produced when the icing is rolled out. Lay the icing over any shells you may have. If you have none at home, you may find that your local fishmonger will give you a few, or sell them to you for next to nothing. Press the icing into any detail on the shell and trim it to the edge with a sharp knife. Allow to dry for at least four hours and then remove. If you have not already coloured the icing, paint in bright and attractive shades.

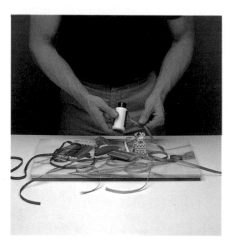

11 Take a number of small gifts, one for each guest at the party, and tie a piece of ribbon round each one, leaving a long tail.

To make the palm tree trunk take 8oz (225g) gelatin icing and roll roughly into a sausage shape about 6″ (7.5cm) long. It should be quite a bit fatter at the bottom than at the top. Using a pointed knife or skewer score 'v' shapes all over the bark of the tree. Leave to dry, for authenticity making a slight bend in the trunk.

SPECIAL FINISHES

To make the palm leaves roll out 4oz (125g) gelatin icing on a work surface lightly dusted with cornflour. Cut out about eight spear-shaped leaves about 2½″ (6.5cm) long. With a sharp knife make a series of ¼″ (5mm) cuts all round the edge like a fringe. Let the leaves dry for at least four hours in the bottom and at the side of a round cake tin, so that they are curved along both their length and their width. When dry paint the trunk brown and the leaves green. Allow to dry for a further two hours. To assemble the tree dab about a teaspoon of royal icing on top of the trunk and press the ends of the leaves into it. If any royal icing is visible when the tree has dried, paint it so that it won't show.

Place the body of the chest on the cake and fix in position with a little royal icing. If you want it to look as though it has partly sunk into the sand, put some fairly stiff royal icing under one end to lift it slightly off the cake. Then take some softer royal icing and smooth it up against the raised side of the chest like a drift of sand. Allow to dry and paint yellow. Allow to dry again. Place the gifts inside the chest with the ribbons trailing out on to the sand. Fill the chest up with gold chocolate money and colourful junk jewellery and lay the lid on top. It is not necessary to fix the lid in place as it will be removed when the gifts are taken out. Fix the tree to the cake behind the chest with stiff royal icing. Place the shells and starfish around the base of the cake. For an added magical effect brush the various items of decoration with several shades of lustre powder.

CANCER STAR SIGN

This cake is made from two packets of cake mix (to make one 7" /18cm round cake) and is therefore very inexpensive, which ties in well with the Cancerian tendency towards frugality. If you prefer you can use a dome-topped bought sponge to avoid the need for carving. The crab's legs are moulded from icing and the body is painted in a good shellfish pink (see p.83) to appeal to Cancer's imagination and well-known sense of fun.

TIMESAVERS

TIMESAVER In this cake you could dispense with the icing altogether, and cover the crab with a layer of white marzipan to provide a sharp background against which to apply colour and decoration. The legs and claws would then also be made out of marzipan.

TIMESAVER A bought sponge cake could be quickly transformed into a crab. Jam sandwich cakes usually come with domed tops, so if you chose to decorate a bought cake you would not have to do any cutting and shaping.

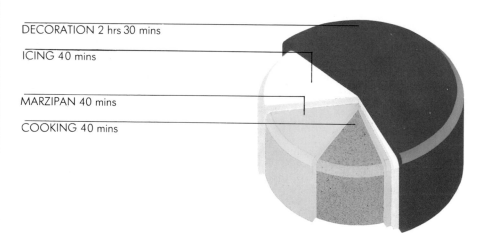

DECORATION 2 hrs 30 mins

ICING 40 mins

MARZIPAN 40 mins

COOKING 40 mins

INGREDIENTS

Decoration
10" (25cm) round cake board
1lb (450g) marzipan
12oz (350g) fondant icing
12oz (350g) gelatin icing
royal icing
apricot jam

Equipment
various food colours
dragees for eyes

1 Make up the cakes according to the instructions on the packet. Allow to cool on a wire rack. Make up the filling according to the instructions. Split the cakes in half and sandwich together with the filling.

2 Make a pattern for the crab shell by tracing out the shape on *p.182* including the decorative sub-divisions of the shell. Cut the cake into the shape of the crab shell using the pattern. Using a sharp knife, shape the cake so that the centre of the top remains the height of the entire cake but then slopes down to the edge, which is about 1½" (4cm) in height.

3 On a work surface lightly dusted with icing sugar roll out 4oz (125g) of the marzipan into a strip 1½" (4cm) wide and long enough to stretch around the cake. To determine the circumference of the shaped cake, wrap a piece of string around the edge and measure its length. Spread the strip with a little apricot jam and fix to the side of the cake. Roll out the remaining 8oz (225g) of marzipan into a circle large enough to cover the cake but extending ¼" (5mm) beyond the edge. Place the pattern on the marzipan as a guide and using a sharp knife cut out the shape of the shell, but this time cutting ¼" (5mm) beyond the edge of the pattern all round. It is not necessary to draw a second pattern as cutting free-hand is quite easy with such a simple shape. Spread the top of the cake with a little apricot jam and fix the marzipan to it.

4 On a work surface lightly dusted with cornflour roll out 4oz (125g) of fondant icing 1½" (4cm) wide and long enough to stretch around the cake. Using a large paintbrush lightly brush the sides of the cake with a little water so that it becomes sticky to the touch, and fix the strip of icing to the side of the cake. Take the remaining 8oz (225g) of fondant icing and roll out into a circle large enough to cover the top of the marzipanned cake and extending ¼" (5mm) beyond the edge of the marzipan. Place the pattern on top of the icing and using a sharp knife cut out the shell shape, but this time cut ½" (1cm) outside the pattern all round. Lay the piece of icing on top of the cake. By extending the marzipan and icing beyond the edge of the cake you will be creating a shell that covers the body of the crab. Allow the icing to dry for about 4 hours before continuing with the decoration.

5 Take 8oz (225g) gelatin icing and divide into 8 1oz (25g) pieces. For the legs, on a work surface lightly dusted with cornflour use your hands to roll out each piece to 3" (7.5cm) long and the thickness of a pencil. With your finger gently roll one end of the piece into a point and cut off the other end neatly. Press into the icing gently with the side of a paintbrush handle or a skewer to divide each leg into 5 sections. Roll the legs back and forth under the paintbrush or skewer to emphasize the divisions and at the same time keep the necessary rounded shape of the leg. Allow the legs to dry in various naturalistic positions as shown for about 4 hours or more if necessary. The painted legs demonstrate the final effect to aim for.

6 Take the remaining 4oz (125g) of gelatin icing and roll out into a sheet about ¼″ (5mm) thick. Cut out two pincer arms as outlined on *p.182*. When each piece has been cut out, gently press on the cut edges to make them slightly rounded. Fix each of the separate pieces together with a little royal icing and allow to dry for 4 hours, or more if necessary.

7 To decorate the cake make up colours of your choice. Take the original pattern as used in step 2 and lay gently on the iced cake. With a cocktail stick trace lightly over the decorative divisions of the shell, scoring into the icing. Obviously the pattern will fall ½″ (1cm) short of the edge. Score around the edge of the pattern to produce a ½″ (1cm) strip all round the edge of the shell. Pick out the scored lines in silver food colour and allow to dry for about 20 minutes. Using the colours of your choice, paint in the various decorative divisions and allow to dry for an hour or so.

8 Further decorations in either silver or another food colour can be added. When the legs and pincers are dry, paint them with one of your chosen food colours and allow to dry. The ½″ (1cm) strip around the edge of the shell can be painted in a third colour. The eyes can be made using either large dragees, or small dragees mounted on circular pieces of icing cut out from any icing remains. Fix to the cake with royal icing.

9 To assemble the cake take each leg in turn and fix to the side of the cake at the cut-off end with royal icing, positioning them under the shell around the back two thirds of the cake. Fix the pincers in position at the sides of the cake just underneath the shell with royal icing.

LEO

Leo's spirited personality will warm to this lionhearted tribute based on two 10" (25cm) round spicy ginger cakes with a stem ginger and cream filling. The three-dimensional lion's face and his mane of flames are moulded from marzipan and applied to the cake under the fondant. The design is copied from an outline on p.184 and the various sections can be filled in with vibrant solid colour or delicate brushwork as in the photograph on p.87.

To make the cake. Grease a 10" (25cm) round cake tin and line with greaseproof paper. Gently heat the golden syrup, black treacle, sugar and butter or margarine in a pan over low heat. Mix well. Sift the flour, spices and bicarbonate of soda into a bowl. Pour the treacle mixture into the flour and mix well. Add the milk and beaten eggs and mix until smooth. Pour into the prepared tin and bake in a preheated oven at 160°C/325°F/Gas mark 3 for 1–1¼ hours. The cake is ready when firm to the touch. A skewer inserted in the centre of the cake should come out clean. Remove the cake from the tin and allow to cool. The cake is best left for 24 hours before being eaten to let the flavours develop.

For the filling, cream the butter or margarine with the sugar and add syrup from the stem ginger to taste.

INGREDIENTS

(for one cake)
6oz (175g) golden syrup
6oz (175g) black treacle
4oz (125g) soft brown sugar
6oz (175g) butter or margarine
12oz (350g) plain flour
4 level teaspoons ground ginger
2 level teaspoons mixed spice
1 level teaspoon bicarbonate of soda
8 fl oz (250ml) milk
4 eggs, beaten

Filling
4oz (125g) butter or margarine
8oz (225g) sifted icing sugar
syrup from stem ginger to taste
chopped stem ginger

Decoration
12" (30cm) round cake board
4lb (1.85kg) marzipan
2lb (900g) fondant icing
apricot jam
a little royal icing

Equipment
metallic gold ribbon
food colours
lustre powder

TIMESAVERS

TIMESAVER It is possible to decorate this cake more simply by using the second Leo outline on p.184 and applying the icing like marquetry or a jigsaw. Marzipan the cake in one flat piece. Make up three colours of fondant icing: pale brown, red and orange. Cover the cake with red icing. Using the second Leo design, cut out the lion's face in pale brown and apply to the cake. Cut out the flame shapes from the orange icing and fix around the lion's face. Paint on the details of the face using the first outline as your guide and finish off by outlining the flames and crown in gold food colour. Dust with lustre powder.

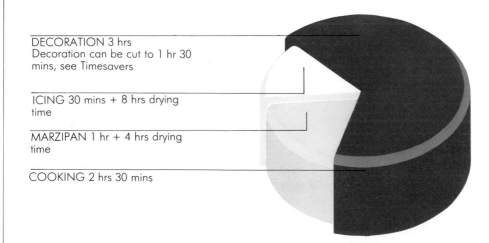

DECORATION 3 hrs
Decoration can be cut to 1 hr 30 mins, see Timesavers

ICING 30 mins + 8 hrs drying time

MARZIPAN 1 hr + 4 hrs drying time

COOKING 2 hrs 30 mins

1 The design for this cake can be found on *p.184*. Trace the complete head and the marzipan cutting guide on to greaseproof or tracing paper, enlarging the design if necessary to fit your cake.

2 Sandwich the cakes together with a layer of filling and pieces of chopped stem ginger.

3 On a work surface lightly dusted with icing sugar roll out 12oz (350g) marzipan. Using the tin in which the cake was baked as a guide, cut out a circle of marzipan to fit the top of the cake. Spread the top with apricot jam and fix the marzipan to it. Wrap a piece of string around the cake to measure its circumference and also measure its height. Roll out 12oz (350g) marzipan and cut a piece to the measurements just taken. Spread the side of the cake with apricot jam and fix the marzipan to it, in two pieces if necessary for easier handling. Allow to dry for a couple of hours.

4 Take the tracing for the marzipan cutting. Roll out 12oz (350g) marzipan and cut out the outer sections of the design as shown. Using the first tracing as a guide, position the marzipan on the top of the cake and fix in place with a little apricot jam. Roll out a further 8oz (225g) marzipan, slightly thicker this time, and cut out the middle section of the design. Place in position and fix with apricot jam. Roll out another 12oz (350g) marzipan, slightly thicker again, and cut out the lion's face. Fix in position with jam.

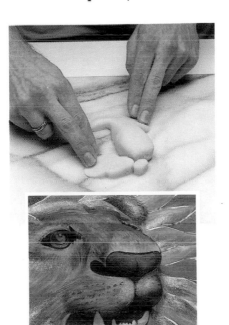

5 For the lion's nose, roll 8oz (225g) marzipan into a ball and flatten the base on your work surface. With a rolling pin, make a slope from the high point of the ball, which should be about 1½″ (4cm) above the work surface. Smooth down the sides so that they slope away from what will become the bridge of the nose. Place your tracing on top of the marzipan and cut out the nose shape as it runs down towards the forehead to include a full eye socket on the left and a part of the eye socket on the right. As the final photograph illustrates, the lion is looking out of the cake at an angle. Take your piece of marzipan and place it in position on the cake. Gently round down the cut edges to blend in with the rest of the face. The slope down from the nose on the right will be sharp as the lion's head is turned to the left. Fix the nose to the cake with apricot jam.

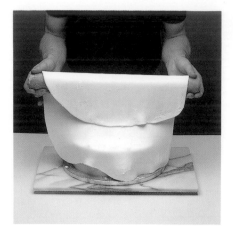

6 On a work surface lightly dusted with cornflour roll out the fondant icing into a sheet large enough to cover the cake. Drape the sheet over the cake and smooth the icing into the sides. Using a flat-bladed knife held against the side of the cake trim off any excess icing.

7 With fingers lightly coated in cornflour gently mould the icing into the marzipan features. Allow to dry for eight hours or overnight. The icing needs to be completely dry before it is painted.

8 Make up a series of red, yellow and orange food colours. Paint the tips of the flames red and then gradually brush into orange and then yellow. Apply the colours one after the other so that they can be merged while still wet. Make some of the flames solid red.

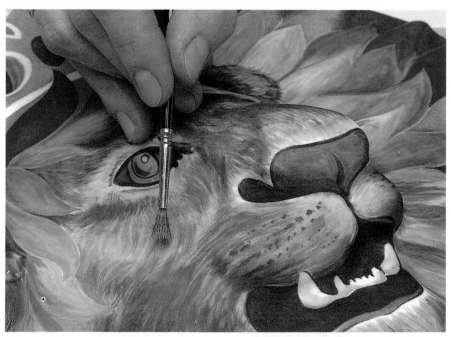

9 Paint the end of the nose and the mouth solid brown, adding a little shading around the lips and on the very tip of the nose. Leave the teeth white, or brush with ivory or palest brown food colour. For the fur, dip a medium paintbrush in brown, splay the bristles out and drag them across the icing. Apply the colour very sparingly, if at all, round the eyes and nose to emphasize these areas. Deeper shades of brown underline the contours of the face and fur merges into flame around it. Pick out the eyes, like the flames, in red, yellow and orange and edge them with a line of unbroken deep brown. Allow the colour to dry completely for several hours.

10 Outline the edges of the flames in gold and fill in the gaps between the outer flames in purple. Paint the crown gold, edged with pale yellow.
The jewels are purple, their facets outlined in silver.

ASSEMBLY

When the paint is dry, dust the surface of the cake with gold lustre powder. Wrap the cake in a wide metallic gold ribbon and secure with a little royal icing.

PISCES

This rich chocolate truffle cake is very quick to make – it needs no cooking. The use of moulds, such as those featured here, opens up an enormous range of possibilities for both cakes and desserts. For a dessert you could leave out the fondant icing and cover the mould instead with a shiny thin layer of chocolate glacé icing. The cakes pictured on p. 91 show the subtle effects that can be achieved with delicate brushwork and a good range of food colours. The two cakes shown here are made from four quantities of chocolate truffle mixture to fill a 9" mould. The amount of the mixture needed will vary according to the size of the mould used.

To make the cake. Break up the chocolate into pieces and put into a bowl along with the butter or margarine. Place the bowl over a pan of gently boiling water. Leave until the chocolate melts, stirring once or twice. Remove the basin from over the pan and stir in the egg yolks, icing sugar, cake crumbs and brandy. Mix thoroughly. Leave to cool for a couple of hours. For a less sweet mixture, you could replace some of the icing sugar with cocoa powder to taste.

INGREDIENTS

Cake (enough for one quantity of mixture)
4oz (125g) plain dessert chocolate
2oz (50g) butter or margarine
2 egg yolks
4oz (125g) sifted icing sugar
4oz (125g) cake crumbs (madeira cake is best)
2 tablespoons brandy (or spirit or liqueur of your choice)

Decoration (for both cakes)
one 18" (46cm) square cake board or two 10" (25cm) square boards
2lb (900g) marzipan
8oz (225g) plain dessert chocolate
1lb (450g) fondant icing
apricot jam

Equipment
fish mould about 9" (23cm) long
food colour

TIMESAVERS

TIMESAVER To avoid painting the fish, knead a number of food colours into the icing, mixing them incompletely so as to create a swirled effect when rolled out. When dry, dust the icing with a number of shades of lustre powder.

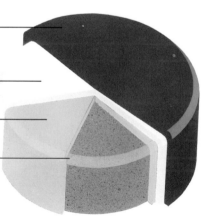

DECORATION 2 hrs
By not painting an hour can be saved, see timesaver

ICING 40 mins

MARZIPAN 40 mins + 2 hrs drying time

PREPARATION 45 mins

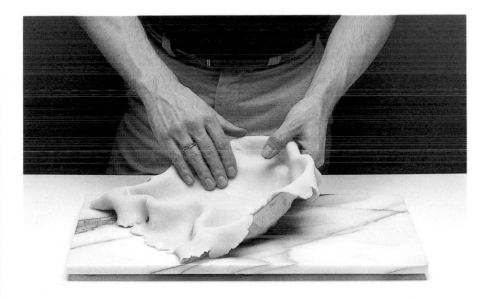

3 Spoon the truffle mixture into the mould, gently pressing down to ensure that there are no holes or gaps in the filling, which should be quite solid. Do not press too hard or you may damage the chocolate coating. Level off the mixture leaving the ¼" (5mm) strip of marzipan uncovered.

1 Take 8oz (225g) marzipan. Roll out on a work surface lightly dusted with cornflour into a sheet large enough to line the mould. Place the marzipan inside the mould and gently press into the detail inside. Trim any excess marzipan to the edge of the mould.

2 Break the chocolate for the decoration into pieces and place in a bowl. Place the bowl over a pan of gently boiling water. Wait until the chocolate melts. Remove the bowl from over the pan and allow to cool for a few minutes. Using a large paintbrush coat the inside of the marzipanned mould with chocolate leaving a ¼" (5mm) strip of marzipan uncovered round the edge. Allow the chocolate coating to dry and harden completely. The layer of hardened chocolate will prevent the moist truffle mixture from wetting the marzipan and thereby making it impossible to turn the cake out of the mould.

4 Smear the surface of the truffle mixture with apricot jam. Roll out 8oz (225g) marzipan into a sheet large enough to cover the mould. Lay the marzipan over the truffle mixture and trim any excess to the edge of the mould. Seal the edges by pressing the sheet of marzipan against the ¼" (5mm) strip left uncovered by the truffle mixture.

5 Turn the cake out of the mould immediately and allow to dry for a couple of hours.

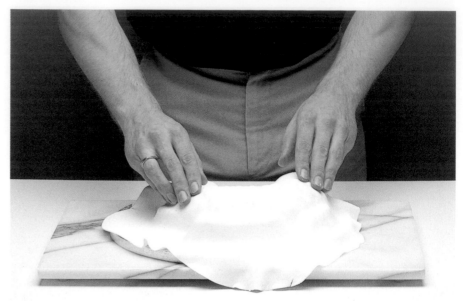

6 On a work surface lightly dusted with cornflour roll out 8oz (225g) fondant icing as thinly as possible so that the maximum amount of detail from the mould will show through when the icing is applied to the cake. Lay the icing over the cake.

7 Gently smooth the icing into the detail on the cake. Using a sharp knife trim any excess icing to the edge of the cake.

Repeat steps 1 to 6 to make the second fish for the completed Pisces cake.

SPECIAL FINISHES

We have chosen to use subtle shades of blue, green and pink washes to colour the fish. Make up several pale colours. Brush on gently, merging the shades into each other. Add edible lustre powder to emphasize the scales and give the fish a silvery sheen, or if lustre powder is not available emphasize the scales with a darker colour.

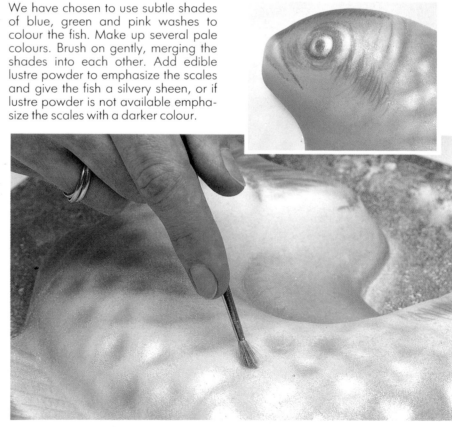

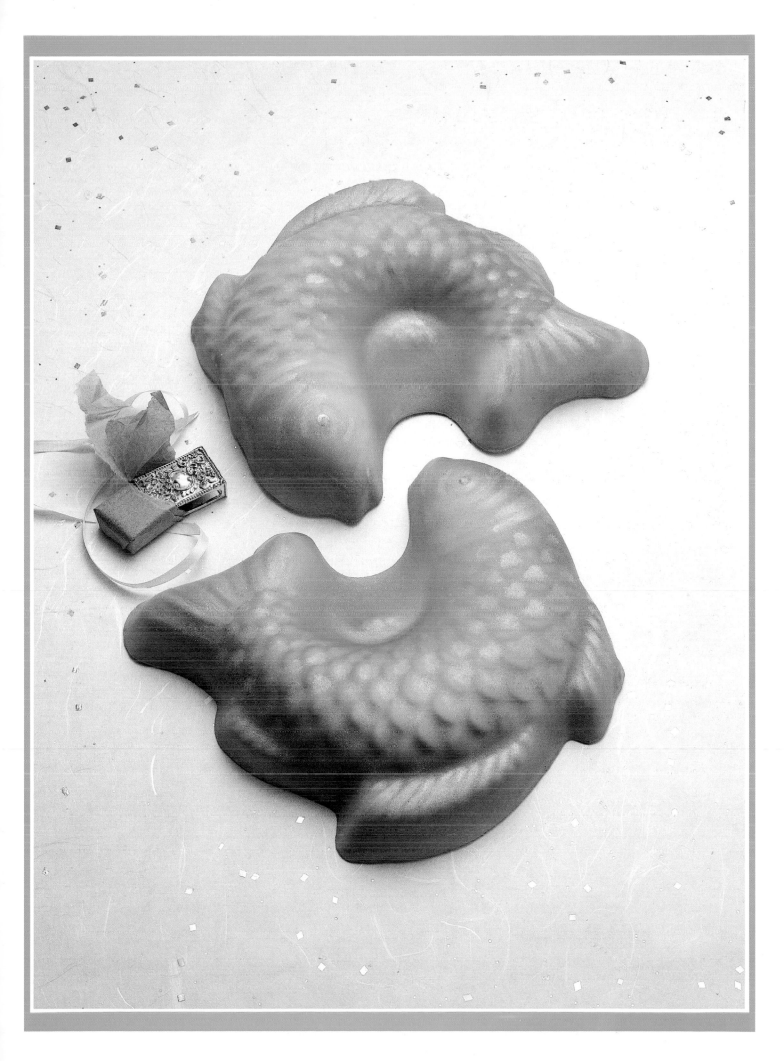

HOT AIR BALLOON

A refreshingly light cake of orange madeira layered with cream and marmalade and flavoured with liqueur forms the basis for this breathtaking wedding centrepiece. You need two 12" (30cm) round cakes and a square cake. The gondola cake requires only basic carving but the balloon, which is hollow, demands a degree of dexterity. It is made in two halves by laying gelatin icing over a mould. The two halves are then fitted together like a box, which could contain small gifts, confetti, orchids or flower petals. Icing run-outs supply relief decoration and delicate brushwork provides the finishing touches.

To make the cake. Cream together the butter or margarine and sugar until light and fluffy. Add the eggs two at a time and mix well followed by a tablespoon of flour. Sift the remaining flour together and fold into the mixture followed by the orange rind and juice. Grease a 12" (30cm) round cake tin and line with greaseproof paper. Spoon the mixture into the prepared tin and level the top. Cook in a preheated oven at 160°C/325°F/Gas mark 3 for the times shown. The cake is ready when risen and firm to the touch. Cool in the tin for 5 minutes. Turn out on to a wire rack to cool completely. Remove the lining paper.

For the filling, cream the butter or margarine into the icing sugar. Mix in the orange rind and juice.

INGREDIENTS

	12" (30cm)	8" (20cm)
	round	square
butter or margarine	1lb (450g)	8oz (225g)
caster sugar	1lb (450g)	8oz (225g)
eggs	8	4
self-raising flour	1lb (450g)	8oz (225g)
plain flour	8oz (225g)	4oz (125g)
grated orange rind	2 oranges	1 orange
orange juice	3 tablespoons (45ml)	4 tablespoons (20ml)
cooking time	1 hour 15 minutes	1 hour 15 minutes

Filling (for the 12"/30cm cake only)
6oz (175g) butter or margarine
1lb (450g) icing sugar
1 teaspoon grated orange rind
2 tablespoons (30ml) orange juice
orange crystal marmalade
liqueur of your choice

Decoration
16" (40cm) round cake board
3lb (1.4kg) marzipan
2lb (900g) blue fondant icing
1lb (450g) white fondant icing
3lb (1.4kg) gelatin icing
apricot jam
royal icing

INGREDIENTS

Equipment
miniature silk bridal flowers
baby ribbon
DAS modelling clay (from art shops)
plastic or wood decorative detail (from hardware shops – sold for embellishing cupboard doors etc.)
mould for the balloon
3 yards (3m) small seed pearls
silk rosebuds, gypsophila, honeysuckle
wire lampshade support about 4" (10cm) high

TIMESAVERS

TIME SAVER The delicate pink shading on the hot air balloon undoubtedly adds to its attraction, but instead of painting this on afterwards you could knead a little pink food colour into the icing before moulding.

TIME SAVER Instead of making a gondola for underneath the balloon, you could bake a 4" (10cm) or 6" (15cm) round madeira cake and make the tub shape into a more traditional looking basket.

TIME SAVER Making the decorative run-outs of icing to surround the monogram and for the swagging is quite time-consuming. You could instead decorate the balloon with small bridal flowers and ribbons.

DECORATION 3 hrs 30 mins + 8 hrs drying time

ICING 1 hr + 4 hrs drying time

MARZIPAN 1 hr 15 mins + 4 hrs drying time

COOKING 1 hr 15 mins per cake

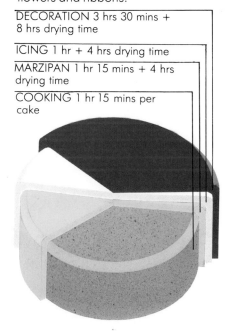

1 Split each cake in half. Sandwich the two halves together with 6oz (175g) orange crystal marmalade. Sprinkle the cakes with the liqueur of your choice. Sandwich the two cakes together with the orange cream filling.

On a work surface lightly dusted with icing sugar roll out 1lb (450g) marzipan. Using the tin in which the cake was baked as a guide, cut out a 12″ (30cm) circle. Spread the top of the cake with apricot jam and fix the marzipan in position. Measure the depth of the cake. Wrap a piece of string round the edge to measure the circumference. Roll out 1lb (450g) marzipan and cut out a strip to the measurements just noted. For ease of handling cut the strip into two halves. Spread the side of the cake with jam and fix the marzipan in position, making the seams as neat as possible. Leave to dry for four hours.

2 On a work surface lightly dusted with cornflour roll out the blue fondant icing into a sheet large enough to cover the cake. Lay it over the cake and smooth down the sides, cutting off the excess with a flat-bladed knife held against the cake. Allow to dry for four hours.

3 Trace the designs for the clouds from *p.185* on to greaseproof paper and cut out. Roll out 1lb (450g) gelatin icing and cut out the cloud shapes in batches of five (see next step).

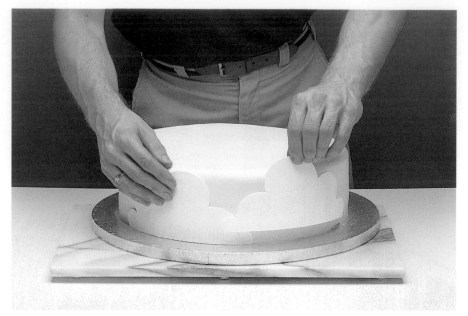

4 Allow the clouds to dry resting against the outside and inside of the tin in which the cake was baked, so that they take on the same curve. Allow to dry for four hours or until completely hard. Make and dry the clouds in batches of five, as no more will fit on the tin.

5 Once the clouds have dried and can stand up, they will be placed round the cake.

6 Mix some pale pink food colouring and paint the clouds as illustrated. There are two methods. The first involves painting simple outlines. The second involves using a close-textured sponge as illustrated in the painting techniques on *p.13*. Here the shadows in the clouds are gently sponged on to give a delicate impression of depth. Allow the colours to dry for an hour.

7 To make your balloon, choose a mould from any that you have available or can buy. The mould used here is an ice cream mould, which was expensive but ideal for the purpose because it is the perfect shape. You could, however, just as well use an Easter egg mould or even a sieve – preferably a new one with a regular rounded shape.

8 To make the balloon roll out 8oz (225g) gelatin icing and lay over the top half of the mould. Working quickly, smooth the icing over the mould and into any detail on it. Trim off any excess to produce a very neat edge half way round the mould. Ideally there should be no signs of creasing in the finished balloon. However, if your icing persists in creasing, try to confine the creases to the top and bottom of the balloon, which will eventually be covered with decoration. Allow the icing to dry for eight hours or overnight. When dry, take the icing off the mould and leave to dry out com-

pletely while you make the second half of the balloon. For the second half, proceed as for the first half, but this time ice the inside of the mould. This may sound a little odd, but it is done for a good reason – to make the two halves fit together by pressing one half just inside the other, like closing a tin. The balloon is thus easier to assemble, and to take apart again, if you should wish. If you are using a sieve, it would be better to make both halves on the outside, and stick them together with royal icing, or one half of the balloon will bear the pattern of the sieve.

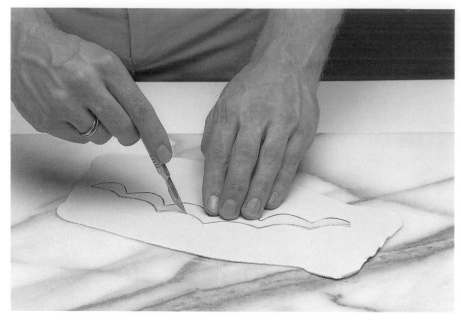

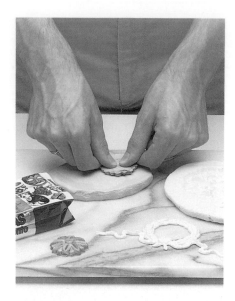

9 Trace the design for the balloon swagging from *p.185* on to a piece of greaseproof and cut out. Take 6oz (175g) gelatin icing and colour pale blue. Cut out a long piece of swagging to go round the wide part of the mould, and a shorter piece to go round the top. Save the leftover icing to make a second set of swagging.

11 Take the packet of DAS modelling clay and, following the instructions, make it soft and roll out into a sheet about ½″ (1cm) thick. Take the plastic or wood decorative detail and push firmly into the clay to leave a clear impression. Remove the detail and let the impression or 'mould' dry. The mould in this case was made from a circular flower pattern about 1½″ (4cm) in diameter and another featuring a laurel wreath and ribbons. Details of this sort are ideal for making unusual icing run-outs.

10 Place the swagging in position on the mould to dry. While it is still soft, pinch the narrow part of the swagging with the end of a brush to draw it up into gentle folds. Let it dry for about four hours. Repeat with a second set of swagging for the other side of the balloon.

12 To make the wreath and ribbon run-out take 6oz (175g) gelatin icing and colour it pale pink. Dust the mould lightly with cornflour and press half the icing into it firmly, making sure that the whole mould has been filled with icing. As soon as you have made the shape, tip the icing out – you may need to pull gently so that it will come away cleanly. Trim any excess icing from the run-out with a sharp knife. Read step 13 before making the other wreath and ribbon run-out.

13 Let the ribbon run-out dry for about four hours in position on the centre of the balloon mould. Repeat step 12 once the first iced detail has dried. To make the circular flower detail take 4oz (125g) gelatin icing and divide into four. Lightly brush the circular mould with cornflour and firmly push the icing into the mould. Immediately remove it and trim off the excess. Allow to dry flat. Repeat to produce four flowers.

14 Cut the square madeira cake into two oblongs measuring 8 × 4″ (20 × 10cm). Place one on top of the other. Trace the side of the gondola from P185 and cut out the pattern. Place the pattern on the side of the cake. Cut a gentle curve at the front and a straight angled line and a step into the back. Finally cut two steps into the top for the seat and trim off any excess cake.

15 Now finish carving the prow of the gondola. Beginning at the front, carve outwards and downwards on both sides, leaving the back of the cake intact. Look closely at the photographs and copy the shape required.

16 To marzipan the gondola make a template of the top of it on tracing paper. Make another template of the side (you may not have followed the tracing you made from *p.185*.very accurately). On a work surface lightly dusted with icing sugar roll out 8oz (225g) marzipan. Cut out the shape of the top of the gondola, extending it about 6″ (15cm) beyond the pattern at the back, so that you will have enough marzipan to cover the stern. Spread the appropriate parts of the cake with apricot jam and fix on the marzipan. Take the remaining 8oz (225g) marzipan, roll it out and cut two sides. Spread the sides of

the cake with apricot jam and fix the marzipan in position. Allow to dry for two hours.

17 Use the same templates for icing the gondola. On a work surface lightly dusted with cornflour roll out 8oz (225g) white fondant icing. Cut out the shape for the top of the gondola, again extending it 6″ (15cm) at the back to cover the stern. Moisten the

marzipan with a little water and fix the icing in position. Roll out the remaining white fondant and cut out two pieces for the sides. Moisten the sides of the cake and fix them on. Gently press all the seams together to make them as neat as possible.

SPECIAL FINISHES

The wire lampshade support that holds the balloon can be bought separately in any lighting department at very little cost. If the one you have bought is too tall, you can cut it down with wire cutters. Wrap the frame in baby ribbon to cover it completely.

Place the clouds at intervals round the side of the cake, fixing them to the board with dabs of royal icing. Fix the two halves of the balloon together. You could add pink shadows to the balloon with a close textured sponge, from top to bottom, as for the clouds. This will emphasize the segments of the balloon. Allow the colour to dry for an hour. If using a monogram, trace the letters from.*p.185*.Transfer to the balloon with graphite paper and paint silver. Allow to dry for an hour. If using, stick the seed pearls to the balloon in lines from top to bottom with dabs of royal icing. Fix the wreath and ribbon run-outs around the monogram with royal icing. Fix the swags in position likewise. Fix one of the circular decorations at the top and the other at the bottom. Additional colour can be added to the swags and wreath as shown – this very simple effect is achieved with pink, blue and silver. Fix miniature silk flowers and lengths of baby ribbon at intervals along the swags. Place the gondola on top of the cake. Place the balloon support on top of the gondola and fix it firmly with stiff royal icing – do not stint on the amount, as it will be hidden under silk flowers. Decorate the support with flowers, ribbons and lengths of seed pearls. Fix one circular decoration to each side of the gondola and decorate further with flowers and ribbon.

PANDA

Three 8″ (20cm) and one 6″ (15cm) round madeira sponges sandwiched with sweetened curd cheese and fruit preserve provide an ideal medium for the detailed and careful cutting and shaping this cake requires. The step-by-step photographs illustrate just how well fine, close-textured cake responds to carving. For sculpting you will need a sharp knife, a steady hand and patience. The application of fondant icing to an irregular shape like this requires a deft touch. The picture of the finished cake on p.107 shows how the panda's black markings cunningly hide any visible seams.

To make the cake. Cream the butter or margarine and sugar together until light and fluffy. Add the eggs one at a time and beat into the mixture. Add a spoonful of flour to the mixture after each egg is incorporated and mix again. Sift the remaining flours together and fold into the creamed mixture followed by the lemon juice. Turn the mixture into a greased and lined tin and level the top. Place in a preheated oven set at 160°C/325°F/Gas mark 3 for the times indicated, or until risen and firm to the touch. Turn out on to a wire cooling rack.

For the filling mix the curd cheese with a little milk or cream to achieve a spreading consistency and sweeten to taste with icing sugar. Split the cakes in half and sandwich together with the sweetened cheese mixture and a layer of fruit preserve.

INGREDIENTS

	(for one cake)	
	8″ (20cm)	6″ (15cm)
butter or margarine	8oz (225g)	4oz (125g)
caster sugar	8oz (225g)	4oz (125g)
eggs	4	2
self-raising flour	8oz (225g)	4oz (125g)
plain flour	4oz (125g)	2oz (50g)
lemon juice	4 teaspoons	2 teaspoons
cooking time	1 hour 20 minutes	1 hour

Filling
2lb (900g) curd cheese
2lb (900g) fruit preserve
icing sugar to taste

Equipment
black food colour
twigs (in this case fennel twigs)
wire for wired leaves

Decoration
10″ (25cm) round cake board
1½lb (675g) marzipan
1½lb (675g) fondant icing
8oz (225g) gelatin icing
apricot jam
a little royal icing

TIMESAVERS

TIMESAVER This is a cake where you should not cut corners if you want your panda to look as good as the one illustrated here. However, if you like the idea of a panda but do not want to embark on carving the madeira cake, you could make a two-dimensional panda by cutting the outline of the animal from a single large cake. Marzipan the cake in the usual way and paint on the black detail or add black fondant icing pieces as in the Flag cake.

To give slightly more body the arms, legs and muzzle could be added as a second layer of marzipan as in the Body Beautiful, and then iced and decorated as just described.

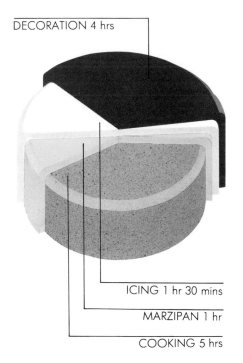

DECORATION 4 hrs

ICING 1 hr 30 mins

MARZIPAN 1 hr

COOKING 5 hrs

1 As this cake requires quite a lot of carving, it is advisable not to overfill each layer. Assemble the cakes as illustrated. Place the 6″ (15cm) cake slightly towards the back of the top 8″ (20cm) cake, so that it is just off-centre. Allow the complete block to rest for 3 or 4 hours before working on it. The separate layers should now not move out of place when handled.

2 Using a sharp kitchen knife, begin carving the panda. Starting at the highest point of the 6″ (15cm) cake, carve a gentle curve from the top to the bottom of the pile of cakes. This curve should be cut into the back of the cakes extending half way round each side. As madeira is quite a close-textured cake it is possible to cut or shave very slim pieces of cake from the block and in this way proceed very slowly until you are satisfied with the shape.

3 At this stage concentrate on carving the general outline of arms, legs and head without being too concerned about the finer details. Use the layers of cake as measures to help you determine the size and position of individual features. For the legs, start at a point half way round each side towards the back of the cake. Take a point at the top of the second layer of cake and with the tip of your knife draw a line down to the top of the first layer in the middle of the front of the cake. Repeat for the other leg. Using the sharp point of the knife cut out a block of cake from the middle of the bottom layer approximately 1½″ (4cm) wide and 1″ (2.5cm) deep. This is the space between the feet. Take your knife and starting with the line that you have drawn, carve upwards and inwards to produce the rounded shape of the legs. Look at the photographs and note how the leg emerges from the shape of the panda's back, growing thicker towards the front, where it is at its thickest. In this photograph you can see where the original line was cut from the top of the second to the top of the first layer – below the line the cake is the golden brown of the cooked outside, and above the line the carving eats into the pale gold of the inside of the cake. Repeat for the other leg.

5 The second stage of making the panda is to carve in more detail, beginning with the head. From the front, the head is roughly triangular in shape. At the back and sides it is carved to join the curve of the back and shoulders. The muzzle and lower half of the head are carved out of the bottom layer of the top cake. On either side of the broad nose, carve hollows for the eyes.

6 Once the head is shaped, gently curve the arms and legs so that the back and sides of the panda are continuous curves.

4 To carve the arms the process is essentially the same as for the legs. To carve the underside of the arms, once again start at a point half way round the side of the back of the cake. Starting at a point on top of the fourth layer of cake, take your knife and draw a line down to the top of the third layer, ending in the centre of the front. Starting from the line just drawn, carve downwards and inwards into the cake. This section of carving will meet up with the upwards and inwards carving that produced the leg, leaving the third layer to be shaped gently into the tummy. To produce the upper edge of the arm, take your kitchen knife and draw a line extending from the top of the fifth layer to the top of the fourth layer in the centre of the front of the cake. Cut out a block of cake between the paws 1¼" (3cm) wide and 1" (2.5cm) deep. Take your knife and carve upwards and inwards from the line just drawn. Check in the photographs to see exactly how the arm emerges from the back of the panda. The arm gets thicker towards the front, reaching its maximum extension from the body at the paws. For the head, start at the highest point on the top cake and cut a gentle slope down to the middle of the front of it.

7 The spaces between the arms and legs and down the front of the cake – the panda's tummy – should be shaped to slope down and out from under the chin to the widest point half way between the arms and legs, and then down and inwards to the bottom of the cake between the legs.

8 Marzipanning the cake is a rather fiddly process and you should not be unduly concerned if the result looks a little untidy. Marzipan is not as malleable as fondant icing, and it is difficult to get it to stretch along two curves at the same time. It is possible to marzipan the panda in three pieces. As illustrated, the first piece should cover the whole of the back and extend half way round each side. Spread the cake with apricot jam. Roll out 12oz (350g) marzipan quite thinly and lay on the cake. Press out as many of the folds and creases as possible and trim the edges with a sharp knife. The second piece of marzipan should be fixed across the panda's chest to meet the first piece at the sides. For this take 8oz (225g) marzipan and roll out thinly. Spread the cake with apricot jam and fix on. Trim the edges with a sharp knife and match the seams as closely as possible. To marzipan the head, spread the remaining cake with apricot jam. Roll out the remaining 4oz (125g) marzipan thinly and apply to the cake. This stage is not straightforward in that the marzipan will fold and crease under the chin. Simply use scissors and a sharp knife to trim away the excess – any slight irregularities will not show in this position. Do not worry if the surface is uneven, or if the marzipan splits a little as it is being smoothed over the carved features. This is almost bound to happen and will not show in the finished panda. Allow to dry for 8 hours.

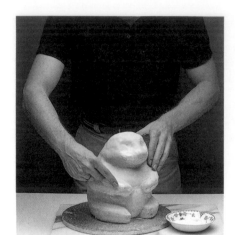

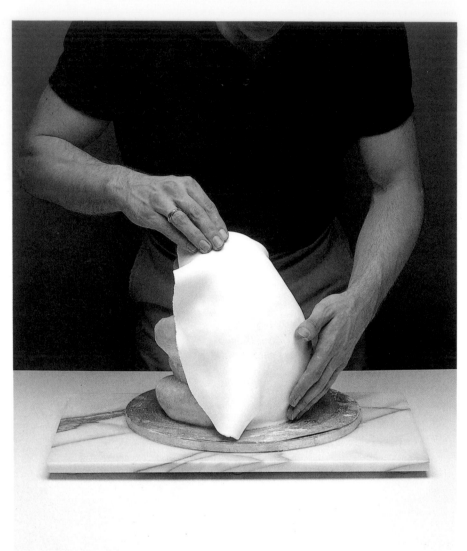

9 Now is the time to correct any bothersome irregularities in the surface of the cake and to mend the splits in the marzipan. Simply take some of the royal icing and smooth it into the problem areas. When this has dried you will have the smooth surface you need in order to proceed.

10 The icing is applied in three stages, as with the marzipan. Brush the marzipan with a little water to make it sticky before applying the icing. On a work surface lightly dusted with cornflour roll out 12oz (350g) of the fondant icing. Moisten the back and sides of the cake and drape the icing sheet over it. Gently smooth the icing as far as possible around the sides of the cake. Trim off and keep the excess. Take special care in trimming and neatening the edge across the top of the panda's head. Icing seams on this particular cake can be disguised under the patches of black fur, but bear in mind that the face, which is white, should not have seams running across it. Moisten the panda's front with water, roll out 8oz (225g) icing and fix across the panda's chest and to just below the chin, meeting the first sheet at the sides. Trim the icing carefully to neaten the side seams. Trim neatly under the chin and keep any leftovers. Finally, ice the head. Moisten the rest of the cake with a little water. Take the remaining icing plus any leftovers and roll out. Drape over the panda's head and gently smooth in the facial detail. Using a sharp knife carefully trim off any excess icing and press the seams together to make them as neat as possible. Allow the icing to dry for at least 2 hours before proceeding.

11 To make the ears take 2oz (50g) gelatin icing and roll into a ball. Press your thumb into the centre of the ball, and then cut in half. Fix to the sides of the head with royal icing. If there are any gaps between the ears and the head fill these in with more royal icing so that the ear is continuous with the head.

13 The detail of the eyes and claws is created by leaving white icing uncovered. As far as possible, cover up the icing seams with black food colour. Allow to dry completely.

12 To colour the panda make up some black food colour and apply to the icing in the areas illustrated. Note that the edges of the black areas are feathered to give the impression of fur – do this by splaying out the bristles of the brush when applying the colour at the edges.

14 To make the bamboo leaves take the remaining gelatin icing and roll into balls the size of a hazelnut. Insert a 3″ (7.5cm) length of modelling wire into each ball and roll out so that the wire extends well into the flattened-out piece. Using a sharp knife, cut out spear-shaped leaves. The leaves can either be allowed to dry flat or can be scored down the centre with a cocktail stick and have each side bent upwards to create a 'v'-shape in cross-section. Allow to dry for about 4 hours, or longer if necessary. Paint them green and allow to dry again. Trim the wire stalks to 1″ (2.5cm) each.

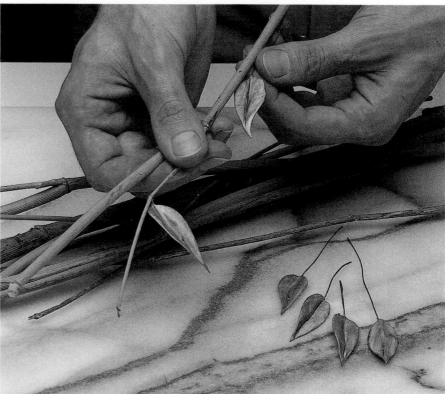

15 Take the fennel twigs (or other twigs you have selected) and glue the wire stalks to them so that the leaves stick out at an angle. This decorative feature is obviously not intended for eating, so this is one instance where glue can safely be used. If you prefer to use royal icing, you will need to colour it once it has dried.

ASSEMBLY

Prop the bamboo between the panda's paws and legs and scatter any remaining twigs and leaves around the base of the cake.

MOUSEHOUSE

The charming mousehouse pictured on p.113 is based on four 9" (23cm) round chocolate and banana cakes layered with banana cream. The irregular tree trunk is made by moulding tree roots in marzipan and fixing them to the cake before the fondant is added. The figure of the mouse is modelled from white marzipan and the windows are cut from gelatin icing. Anyone who enjoys painting will take great pleasure in decorating this cake. An additional feature of a flowerpot roof can be made by moulding gelatin icing onto a plastic plant pot.

To make the cake. Cream the butter and sugar together until light and fluffy. Beat in the honey, then the eggs one at a time. Mix in the mashed banana. Sift the flour and cocoa together and fold into the mixture. Grease a 9" (23cm) round cake tin and line with greaseproof paper. Spoon the mixture into the prepared tin and level the top. Cook in a preheated oven at 160°C/325°F/Gas mark 3 for about 45 minutes or until firm to the touch. Turn out of the tin and allow to cool.

For the filling, cream together the butter or margarine and icing sugar, adding banana flavouring to taste.

INGREDIENTS

(for one cake)
4oz (125g) butter or margarine
4oz (125g) caster sugar
1 tablespoon clear honey
2 eggs
1 banana, mashed
5oz (150g) self-raising flour
3 tablespoons cocoa powder

Filling
12oz (350g) butter or margarine
2lb (900g) icing sugar
a few drops of banana flavouring

Decoration
12" (30cm) round cake board
4½lb (2kg) yellow marzipan
2½lb (1.1kg) gelatin icing
3lb (1.4kg) fondant icing
8oz (225g) white marzipan
apricot jam
royal icing made with 1 egg white

Equipment
food colour
lustre powder
6" (15cm) high plastic plant pot
modelling wire in 3" (7.5cm) lengths
artificial stamens

TIMESAVERS

TIMESAVER Wiring the leaves provides you with a better means of displaying them, but if you prefer, you could leave out the wire and just stick the leaves to the cake with dabs of royal icing.

TIMESAVER The windows and window boxes on the mousehouse are charming but quite fiddly to make. To save time, when brushing the tree trunk with brown food colour leave the space for the windows white and then paint on the details of the curtains and the leaded panes later.

TIMESAVER If you have no time to make the wired bunches of flowers, you could use dried flowers, wheat, barley and grasses, which would give an added touch of authenticity.

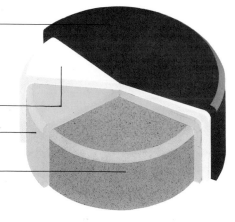

DECORATION 4 hrs + 8 hrs drying time
Up to 1 hr 30 mins can be saved on decoration, see Timesavers

ICING 1 hr + 4 hrs drying time

MARZIPAN 1 hr + 4 hrs drying time

COOKING 45 mins per cake

1 Spread the filling on the cakes and pile one on top of the other.

2 Using a long-bladed kitchen knife cut a gentle slope into the top cake. Cut thin irregular slices off the sides of the cake – this will be the basis for the tree trunk. Decide which face of the cake will be the front. Cut a slice off the front of the cake leaving it smooth and vertical so that the door will fit neatly on to it.

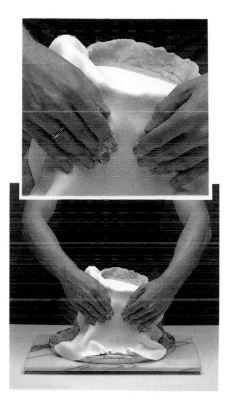

3 Take three separate pieces of yellow marzipan weighing 12oz (350g) each and roll each piece into a rough sausage shape. Press firmly on to the sides of the cake and on to the board to represent the tree's roots.

4 On a work surface lightly dusted with icing sugar roll out 12oz (350g) yellow marzipan. Spread the sides of the cake not already covered with marzipan with apricot jam. Cut the marzipan into pieces and press into the areas between the roots just applied. It is not necessary to be exact or very neat as the tree trunk should have a rough surface.

Take 8oz (225g) yellow marzipan and roll it into a sausage shape. Spread the edge of the top of the cake with apricot jam and fix the marzipan round it. Pinch the marzipan to create a raised collar effect all round the cake. Roll out a further 8oz (225g) marzipan into a rough circle. Spread the top of the cake with apricot jam and fix on the circle, pressing the edges to join the raised collar. Allow to dry for four hours.

5 Moisten one third of the side of the cake with water to make the marzipan sticky. On a work surface lightly dusted with cornflour roll out 1lb (450g) fondant icing into a large sheet. Drape over the moistened section of the cake and press gently onto the marzipan. Cut off excess icing with a sharp knife and keep in cling film. Repeat with the other two thirds. Press the seams together as neatly as possible. It is not essential that they should be vertical. Moisten the top of the cake and roll out the leftover fondant icing into a circle. Drape it over the top of the cake and press down gently so that it covers the top and the collar. Cut off any excess. Allow to dry for four hours.

TIPS

If you would prefer not to use the large quantity of marzipan we suggest for this cake, you could make the tree roots and the 'collar' on top of the tree trunk out of the pieces of cake you have carved away. Stick them in position on the tree trunk with apricot jam.

6 Take the plant pot and make a paper pattern to fit it following the instructions in steps 2 and 3 of the Champagne Celebration on *p. 35*. On a work surface lightly dusted with cornflour roll out 8oz (225g) gelatin icing. Stand the pot on the icing and cut out a circle round the bottom. Place the paper pattern on the icing and cut around. Place the icing shape on top of the pattern and use the paper to wrap the icing round the pot. Tape the paper pattern together to hold the icing in position to dry. Press the icing gently into the pot and leave overnight.

8 To make the chimney take 4oz (125g) yellow marzipan and roll out to a thickness of ½" (1cm). Cut out a rectangle measuring 2 × ¾" (5 × 2cm). Cut out a second rectangle measuring 1 × ½" (2.5 × 1cm). Roll out any marzipan remains into a cylinder of pencil thickness. Cut one piece ¾" (2cm) long and another ½" (1cm) long. Fix the chimney together with royal icing as illustrated and allow to dry for two hours. To decorate paint in brown food colour or in several shades to represent brickwork.

9 To make the windows roll out 6oz (175g) gelatin icing and cut out six rectangles 2 × 1½" (5 × 4cm). Set three aside and cut two smaller rectangles out of each of the other three to make a window frame and two open window panes. Leave the pieces to dry, then assemble as shown, sticking the frames and panes on to the window pieces with royal icing.

To decorate the windows make up brown and blue food colours. Paint the window frames and the leaded panes brown and the curtains inside the windows blue.

7 When dry remove the paper and take off the iced pot. Fix the bottom on the pot with royal icing. Allow to dry. Mix brown and red food colours to make terracotta. Paint the pot all over, splaying out the bristles of the brush to achieve a stippled effect.

10 To make the front door-step roll out 4oz (125g) yellow marzipan to a thickness of ½" (1cm) and cut out a circle about 2½" (6.5cm) in diameter. Cut off a slice from the back of the circle and allow to dry for two hours. Paint all over with brown food colour and allow to dry.

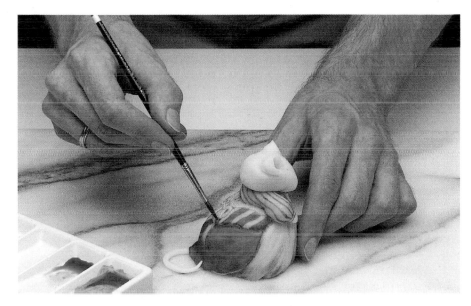

11 To make the skirt for the mouse take 4oz (125g) white marzipan and roll into a rough ball. Press down gently to flatten the bottom of the ball and pinch the back to elongate it slightly. Use the end of a paint-brush to score lines into the marzipan to represent folds in the pinafore and skirt. Allow to dry for one hour. To make the arms take 2oz (50g) white marzipan and roll into a sausage about 2½" (6.5cm) long. Gently pinch the ends and bend down to make paws. Press the middle of the piece to flatten the top and bottom so that it sits comfortably on top of the skirt. Allow to dry for an hour. To make the head take 1oz (25g) white marzipan. Shape to form the nose and pinch to make ears. Hollow out the ears with the end of a paintbrush. Roll the remaining marzipan into a 2" (5cm) tail. Allow to dry for an hour. Assemble the mouse as shown.

12 To paint the mouse make up a series of food colours of your choice. Paint the pinafore with streaks to represent folds in the material. The blouse is painted in stripes to provide contrast, though a third solid colour would also look good.

13 To achieve the effect of bark on the tree trunk, be-gin by painting it all over with a wash of mid brown. Paint the de-tail with a medium brush and a darker brown, splaying out the bristles to leave a trace of fine lines. An additional wash of moss green in places gives a real wood-land feel. Paint the top in a of series circles, starting at the centre and working out. Paint a number of fine lines radiating out from the centre and leave to dry for four hours or until completely dry.

14 To make a toadstool take 6oz (175g) gelatin icing and roll into a rough ball shape. On a work surface lightly dusted with cornflour press the ball gently to flatten the bottom and pinch the top into a good thick stalk. Lay the toadstool upside down and with a sharp knife score fine lines into the underside of the toadstool radiating out from the stalk. Cut small v shapes into the edge of the toadstool at intervals to make a slightly irregular shape. Curve the top upwards as shown and allow to dry for four hours. Make up red and orange food colours and paint the toadstool. Allow to dry.

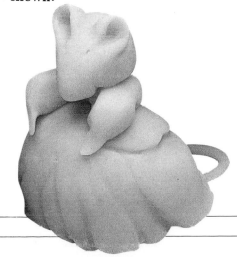

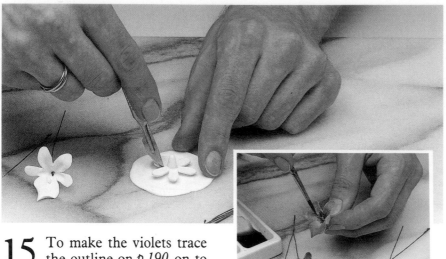

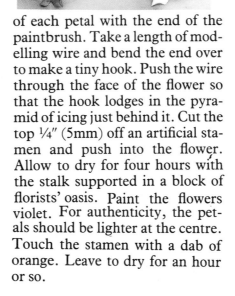

15 To make the violets trace the outline on *p.190.* on to greaseproof paper and transfer to a piece of thin card with graphite paper. Cut out the shape and cut a hole about ¼" (5mm) in diameter out of the centre. Take 4oz (125g) gelatin icing and break off a piece the size of a hazelnut. Roll into a ball and pinch the centre into a pyramid about ½" (1cm) high. Flatten the icing around the pyramid on to the work surface and put the pattern over it so that the pyramid sticks up through the hole. Cut round the flower pattern and remove the paper. Pinch the petals between thumb and forefinger to make them thin and delicate. Push the end of a medium paintbrush into the centre of the flower to hollow it out. Indent the centre of each petal with the end of the paintbrush. Take a length of modelling wire and bend the end over to make a tiny hook. Push the wire through the face of the flower so that the hook lodges in the pyramid of icing just behind it. Cut the top ¼" (5mm) off an artificial stamen and push into the flower. Allow to dry for four hours with the stalk supported in a block of florists' oasis. Paint the flowers violet. For authenticity, the petals should be lighter at the centre. Touch the stamen with a dab of orange. Leave to dry for an hour or so.

16 To make the primroses, take a further 4oz (125g) gelatin icing and proceed as for the violets, using a primrose cutter. Allow the completed flowers to dry for four hours before painting.

17 Paint the primroses yellow, shading the petals so that they are darker at the edges. Paint the stamens yellow and allow to dry.

18 To make the door take 2oz (50g) gelatin icing and roll out on a work surface lightly dusted with cornflour. The door is 2½" (6.5cm) wide at the bottom and 2½" (6.5cm) tall at its highest point. Cut out the door and allow to dry for four hours. Paint with a wood grain effect as described To make the carpet take 2oz (50g) gelatin icing and roll out. Cut out a rectangle 3" × 2" (7.5 × 5cm). Allow the icing to dry in position over one of the roots of the tree for four hours. Paint with food colours in a bright pattern. Allow to dry. Spread the board with a thin layer of royal icing and roughen the surface a little by pricking it with a cocktail stick. On the pathway up to the front door, score several irregular squares into the icing to represent paving stones. Allow the icing to dry for an hour. Paint it green for the grass and pick out the paving stones in yellow and orange. Allow to dry.

ASSEMBLY

Stick the doorstep and door in position with royal icing. Fix the plant pot and chimney to the cake in the same way. Stick the ivy leaves to the side of the cake, with one piece growing round the door. Fix the mouse, carpet and toadstool in position. Twist the wires of the violets and primroses together to make small bunches and dot around the base of the tree.

SPORTS BAG

This simply decorated cake makes a perfect vehicle for a present of small items of sports equipment such as tennis balls, socks and wristbands. Based on two 10″ (25cm) gingerbread cakes with honey cream filling (see the picture on p.119), this design could easily be transformed into a golf bag lying on its side with icing golf club heads on dowelling rods sticking out of it and real golf balls spilling from its mouth.

To make the cake. Grease and line one 10″ (25cm) square tin with greaseproof paper.

Sift the flour and soda into a bowl. Place the butter or margarine, honey, treacle, sugar, syrup, spices and milk in a saucepan and heat gently. Cool slightly and beat in the eggs. Pour the mixture into the flour a little at a time and beat well with each addition. Pour into the tin and bake in a preheated oven at 160°C/325°F/Gas mark 3 for 1 hour to 1 hour 10 minutes or until firm to the touch. Turn out on to a wire rack to cool.

For the filling, cream together the butter or margarine and icing sugar. Add the honey and mix together.

TIMESAVERS

TIMESAVER Save time here by omitting the marzipan pocket detail on the sides of the bag. The sports logo could also be omitted or replaced with a club badge or football rosette stuck to the side of the cake with royal icing.

DECORATION 1 hr 45 mins +
2 hrs drying time
Up to 45 mins can be cut from
the decoration time, see
Timesavers

ICING 1 hr 30 mins + 1 hr
drying time

MARZIPAN 1 hr + 4 hrs drying
time

COOKING 1 hr 10 mins per cake

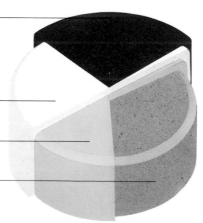

INGREDIENTS

(for one cake)
1lb (450g) plain flour
1 teaspoon bicarbonate of soda
8oz (225g) butter or margarine
8 tablespoons clear honey
8 tablespoons black treacle
4oz (125g) soft brown sugar
4 tablespoons golden syrup
6 teaspoons ground ginger
1 teaspoon ground cinnamon
8 fl oz (240ml) milk
4 eggs

Filling
1½lb (675g) icing sugar
10oz (300g) butter or margarine
2 tablespoons honey

Decoration
12″ (30cm) round cake board
2¾lb (1.25kg) marzipan
2lb (900g) cream coloured
fondant icing
1½lb (675g) pale blue fondant
icing
1lb (450g) gelatin icing
apricot jam
royal icing

Equipment
food colours
sports equipment such as socks,
wristbands, tennis balls
small towel or flannel

1 Cut each cake into two rectangles measuring 10″ × 5″ (25 × 13cm). Sandwich the cakes together with the filling.

2 Using a sharp knife, trim off all the corners and edges to produce a shape like a loaf of bread.

3 Measure the height of the cake. On a work surface lightly dusted with icing sugar roll out 12oz (350g) marzipan and cut out two pieces about 5″ (13cm) wide and to the height of the cake. Spread the ends of the cake with apricot jam and fix on the marzipan. Take a piece of string and wrap over the cake to determine the length of the piece of marzipan needed to cover the rest of the cake. Roll out 1lb (450g) marzipan and cut a piece 10″ (25cm) wide and the length you have measured. Spread the remainder of the cake with jam and fix on the marzipan, pressing it gently on to the cake and getting the seams as neat as possible. Allow to dry for two hours.

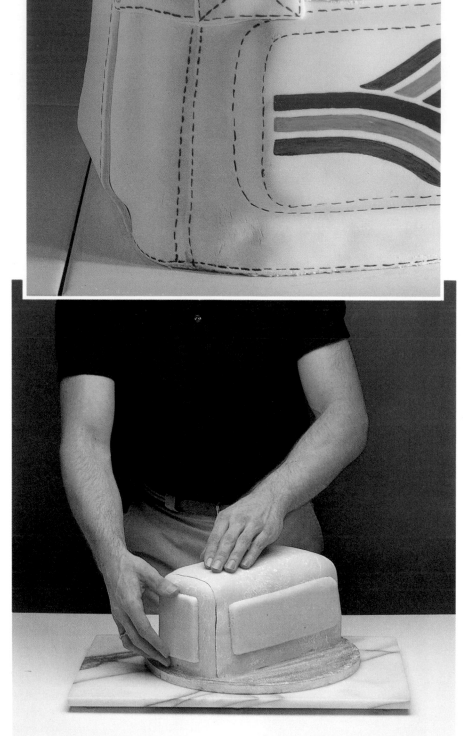

4 To make the side pockets roll out 8oz (225g) marzipan into a sheet about ½″ (1cm) thick. Cut out two rectangles about 3 × 4″ (7.5 × 10cm). Round off the edges by pressing with your fingers. Spread the pieces with jam and fix to each end of the cake.

5 To make the pocket for the front of the bag roll out 8oz (225g) marzipan into a sheet about ½″ (1cm) thick. Cut out a rectangle 8 × 3″ (20 × 7.5cm). Press the edges down to round them off. Spread with apricot jam and fix to the front of the cake. Allow to dry for at least two hours.

6 To ice the cake, measure the width and height of the ends of the cake. Take 12oz (350g) of the cream coloured fondant icing and roll out on a work surface lightly dusted with cornflour. Cut out two rectangles to the measurements just noted. Moisten the marzipan at the ends of the cake by brushing lightly with water. This will help the icing stick. Gently smooth the icing in place and over the pocket detail. Measure the width of the marzipan piece still to be iced and wrap a piece of string over the cake to determine its length. Roll out 1¼lb (600g) of the cream fondant icing and cut a piece to fit. To make handling easier, you can cut this piece in half so that the seam runs along the centre of the top of the bag (where a zip would be). Moisten the marzipan as before and fix on the icing, making sure that the seams are neat with edges closely pressed together. Let the icing dry for an hour or so.

7 Trace the design for the side of the bag from *p.188.* Hold it against the front pocket and score the design lightly into the icing with a cocktail stick. After resting for an hour the icing will still be quite soft and only the faintest impression is necessary. Make up food colours of your choice and paint on the design. Allow to dry and leave the icing to harden for about four hours.

8 The top of the bag is to be filled with sports equipment such as wristbands, socks and tennis balls. These can be real items (as here), and form part of the gift, or they can be made out of icing. In which case, take 4oz (125g) gelatin icing and roll out. Cut out two sock shapes, fold them up as with a real pair, press indentations into the ankles for the ribbing and allow to dry. Take a further 4oz (125g) gelatin icing and roll into a ball. Allow to dry. The ball will dry with a flat bottom, but this will not be seen inside the bag. When dry paint the ball with the characteristic seam. To make a piece of soap and wristbands, take another 4oz (125g) gelatin icing. Form half of it into the shape of a bar of soap. The wristbands are simply rectangles of icing, though as with the other decorations additional colours and patterns can be added for extra interest. Allow the pieces to dry for two hours. Note that this does not include the towel, which will be made in step 9.

9 Fix the iced or real sports equipment to the top of the cake with a little royal icing. To make the opening of the bag, roll out 12oz (350g) blue fondant icing on a work surface lightly dusted with cornflour. Cut out two rectangles about 14 × 4″ (35 × 10cm). Take one of these pieces and moisten one of the long edges. Fix to the side of the cake as illustrated, allowing the icing to fall gently against the sports equipment. Fold the top edge back a little so that the things inside can be seen. Now roll out 4oz (125g) gelatin icing for the towel and cut a square as large as possible. Fold it loosely and place on top of the bag, draping it over the opening. Take the second piece of blue icing and apply to the other side of the cake as for the first piece. Take 4oz (125g) blue fondant icing, roll out and cut two rectangles 3 × 2″ (7.5 × 5cm). Moisten and fix these tabs to the ends of the cake.

10 To make the handle, roll out 8oz (225g) blue fondant icing into a long strip and cut out two pieces about 1 × 18″ (46 × 2.5cm). Moisten both ends of each piece and fix in position on the bag, making sure that the handles do not obscure the detail inside. Allow the icing to dry for four hours.

ASSEMBLY

With blue and silver food colour paint the stitching on the sides of the bag and the zip at the opening.

THREE-TIERED WEDDING CAKE

The classically decorated three-tiered wedding cake pictured on p. 129 would easily serve a party of 200 guests. The soft fondant icing on the rich fruit cake allows for effortless cutting by the bride and groom, and the decoration includes not only delicate icing roses and stephanotis that can be kept as a reminder of a splendid day, but also real flowers to match those chosen for the wedding.

To make the cake. Grease the cake tin and line with a double layer of greaseproof paper. Mix together the dried fruit, quartered cherries and mixed peel in a bowl or plastic bag. Add the almonds, spices and half the flour. Mix the ingredients in the bowl or toss in the plastic bag to coat the fruit with the flour, spice and almonds. Cream the butter and margarine or sugar until light and fluffy. Do not overbeat or the cake will be heavy. Add the eggs one or two at a time and mix well, adding a tablespoon of flour after each egg. Fold in any flour remaining and then add the dried fruit mixture.

Spread the mixture in the tin and level off the top. Some people advise making a slight hollow in the centre of the cake with the back of a spoon so that when cooked, the top of the cake is flat. However, if it is cooked slowly and gently this is not strictly necessary.

Tie two or three thicknesses of brown paper or newspaper round the tin and bake in a preheated oven at 150°C/300°F/Gas mark 2 for the time shown. For the larger cakes it may be advisable to turn down the oven to 140°C/275°F/Gas mark 1 after half the cooking time, and to cover the tin with a double layer of paper or cooking foil to prevent the surface from overcooking. To test for readiness insert a skewer into the centre of the cake. If it is done, the skewer will come out clean. If it is not ready, the skewer will be sticky and have bits of cake mixture sticking to it. When cooked, allow the cake to cool in the tin.

Turn the cake out of the tin and prick the surface all over with a cocktail stick. Spoon brandy or whisky over the cake and then wrap in a double thickness of greaseproof paper and cooking foil. The 'feeding' with brandy or whisky can be repeated at intervals until the cake is decorated. Opinions as to the length of time the cake needs to mature differ from three weeks to several months. Generally speaking the cake will improve somewhat if left for a few months in a cool place, but it is not essential to leave it so long.

TIMESAVERS

TIMESAVER To create the three-tiered wedding cake that we have designed will undoubtedly take a considerable amount of time – time well spent for such a special occasion. The cake will provide a centrepiece for the wedding breakfast and the detachable decorations can be kept as a souvenir. If you should want to cut down on the decoration time, instead of moulding the stephanotis and wired rosebuds, use more real flowers in the trailing decoration to reflect those in the bouquets or headdresses. Or, cut down on the decoration for the bottom tier by emphasizing three individual groups of moulded and real flowers to be placed between the ends of the trailing decorations, instead of joining up the flowers round the baseboard to form a wreath.

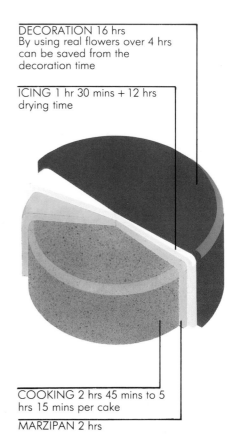

DECORATION 16 hrs
By using real flowers over 4 hrs can be saved from the decoration time

ICING 1 hr 30 mins + 12 hrs drying time

COOKING 2 hrs 45 mins to 5 hrs 15 mins per cake

MARZIPAN 2 hrs

INGREDIENTS

	8″ (20cm)	10″ (25cm)	12″ (30cm)
mixed dried fruit	1lb 5oz (600g)	2lb 6oz (1kg)	4lb 4oz (1.9kg)
glacé cherries	3oz (75g)	5oz (150g)	10oz (300g)
mixed peel, chopped	2oz (50g)	4oz (125g)	7oz (200g)
ground almonds	2oz (50g)	4oz (125g)	7oz (200g)
ground cinnamon	¾ teaspoon	1½ teaspoons	2½ teaspoons
ground mixed spice	½ teaspoon	1 teaspoon	1½ teaspoons
plain flour	7½oz (210g)	14oz (400g)	1½lb (675g)
butter or margarine	6oz (175g)	12oz (350g)	1lb 5oz (600g)
soft brown sugar	6oz (175g)	12oz (350g)	1lb 5oz (600g)
eggs (size 2)	3	6	11
cooking time	2¾ hours	3¾ hours	5¼ hours

Equipment
8 cake pillars
dowelling
modelling wire
food colour
real or silk flowers:
irises
bluebells
sweet peas
gypsophila
baby ribbon
4m (4 yards) 2″ (5cm) wide
ribbon

Decoration
one 16″ (40cm) round cake
board
one 12″ (30cm) round cake
board
one 10″ (25cm) round cake
board
4lb (1.8kg) tragacanth or gelatin
icing
8lb (3.75kg) marzipan
5lb (2.3kg) cream coloured
fondant icing
apricot jam

1 Steps 1 to 8 are the same for all three tiers of the cake. Turn the cake upside down. Roll out a sausage shape of marzipan. You will need 1lb (450g) for the bottom tier, 12oz (350g) for the middle tier and 8oz (225g) for the top tier. Push the marzipan into the gap between the cake and the board.

2 Using a flat-bladed knife trim the marzipan to the edge of the cake. Smooth the marzipan to ensure that the sides of the cake are completely flat.

3 At this stage it is a good idea to check that the top of the cake is level with a spirit level – you may have made it uneven by forcing marzipan under the bottom of the cake. If there is any irregularity, insert more marzipan to compensate. The use of a spirit level is not essential, but it is worth taking the time to get things right at this stage given all the effort you are going to be putting in.

TIPS

If you don't own a spirit level, shown in the picture above, a simpler method of checking if the top of your cake is level is to place a shallow dish or baking tray on the cake and pour in a small amount of water (enough to cover the bottom). Any deviation in level can be spotted – if the water level is not consistent from one side of the dish to the other, the cake is not level.

4 Spread the top of the cake with apricot jam. On a work surface lightly dusted with icing sugar roll out the marzipan. You will need 2½lb (1.1kg) for the bottom tier, 2lb (900g) for the middle tier and 1¼lb (575g) for the top tier. Using the tin in which the cake was baked, cut out a circle of marzipan and place on top of the cake. Measure the circumference of the cake with a piece of string. Cut the string in half. Roll out the marzipan left after the top is in position. Measure the depth of the cake and cut out two rectangles of marzipan to the depth of the cake and the length of the pieces of string. Spread the sides of the cake with apricot jam. Apply the marzipan to the sides of the cake. Press the seams gently together to make them as neat as possible. Using a plastic smoother, gently smooth the marzipan on the sides and top of the cake to make all the seams as even as possible.

5 On a work surface lightly dusted with icing sugar roll out the fondant icing. You will need 2½lb (1.1kg) for the bottom tier, 1½lb (675g) for the middle tier and 1lb (450g) for the top tier. Roll the icing into a circle large enough to cover the cake.

6 With fingers lightly covered in cornflour smooth the icing into the edges of the cake.

8 Cut a piece of ribbon to go round the side of the cake. Cut the end decoratively as illustrated. Fix the ribbon to the side of the cake with a dab of royal icing.

7 Using a flat-bladed knife with the blade lightly pressed against the side of the cake, cut off any excess icing. Leave to dry for 12 hours or overnight.

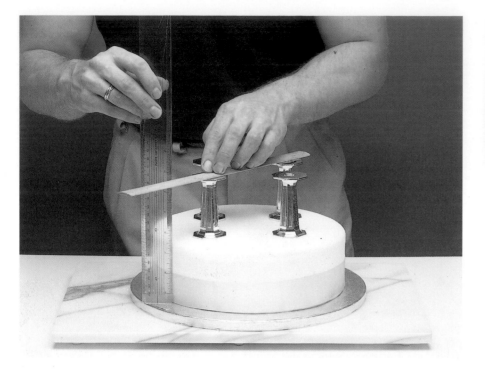

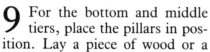

9 For the bottom and middle tiers, place the pillars in position. Lay a piece of wood or a ruler across the top of the pillars. Measure the height from the board to the top of the pillar.

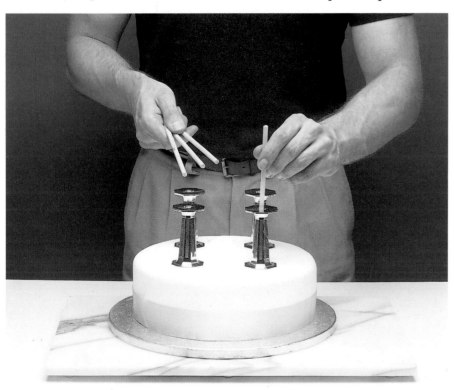

10 Cut four pieces of dowelling to the measurement just taken.

11 With the pillars in position on the surface of the cake, insert the dowelling. If you have miscalculated and the dowelling is too long, take it out and shave off any excess with a sharp knife.

12 Take 1½lb (675g) of the tragacanth or gelatin icing. Roll out half of it and cut out about a dozen ivy leaves. Leave some to dry over a curved surface such as a rolling pin, and allow others to dry flat. Cut the modelling wire into 3″ (7.5cm) lengths. Take the other half of the icing and remove a piece the size of a hazelnut. Insert the wire into it. Roll out the icing leaving the wire running through its centre and cut out an ivy leaf shape. Make about 50 wired leaves. Keep any leftover icing and knead again. Wrap the icing in cling film and use to make more leaves or keep for the rosebuds.

13 Allow the wired leaves to dry over a rolling pin. When dry, paint all the leaves green and allow to dry.

14 Take the flat ivy leaves and place on top of the bottom and middle tiers between the pillars as shown.

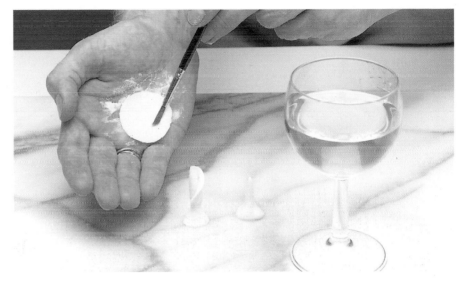

15 When making the roses it is helpful to have a real rose to study so that you make the flower as authentic as possible. Take 1lb (450g) of gelatin or tragacanth icing and colour a pale shade of lemon. This amount of icing should produce between 12 and 16 roses. Take a piece of icing the size of a hazelnut and mould into a small elongated pyramid. Take a second piece of icing of similar size and press out as thinly as possible into a petal shape as illustrated. Moisten the bottom half of the petal with a little water and wind it around the pyramid shape. Gently bend back the edge of the petal as illustrated.

16 The next layer of the rose has three petals, each slightly larger than the one before. Moisten the bottom half of the petal and fix on to the bud. Gently curl back the petals.

17 The final layer of the rose has four or five petals depending on the fullness of bloom required. The petals are essentially the same shape as that illustrated in step 15.

19 On the bottom tier fix two roses at four intervals round the board with a little royal icing.

18 Once the petals are attached to the flower, bend them back, or pinch them to a point as illustrated. Leave the completed rose to dry for 12 hours or overnight. Using a sharp knife cut away the base that will have developed on the completed rose.

20 Arrange the ivy leaves and iris heads as shown.

21 Fill in the gaps between the roses and irises with sweet peas and bluebells.

22 Take 12oz (350g) tragacanth or gelatin icing. Break off a piece the size of a hazelnut and flatten the edges out on to a work surface leaving a central elongated pyramid or stem extending upwards about 1" (2.5cm).

23 Place a stephanotis or five-point star cutter over the stem and press out the flower head.

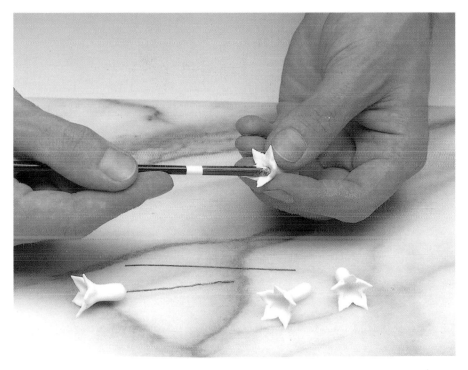

24 Insert the end of a thin paintbrush or skewer into the centre of the flower head and roll backwards and forwards over each petal point to thin it out and produce a curve in the petal. Cut pieces of modelling wire about 3" (7.5cm) long and insert through the flower head and down the stem. Leave about ½" (1cm) wire inside the flower. Leave the stephanotis to dry with the stem pushed into a block of oasis. Make about 36 stephanotis.

25 To make wired rosebuds use the remaining 12oz (350g) tragacanth or gelatin icing coloured a similar shade to the full-blown roses. Make the buds as for the first stage of the rose, but push a 3" (7.5cm) piece of wire into the central pyramid of icing. Like the stephanotis, the rose-buds are best left to dry with their stems pushed into a block of oasis. Make about 36 rosebuds.

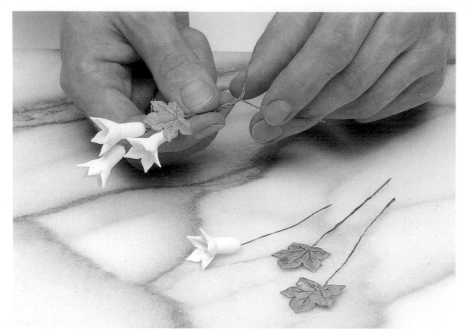

26 To make the three flower garlands, twist the wire stems of the stephanotis, ivy leaves and rosebuds together at intervals.

28 Take the three completed garlands and twist the top ends together to produce one decoration.

29 Make bows as illustrated with baby ribbon, securing the ends with either cotton or modelling wire.

ASSEMBLY

Decorate the side of the middle tier as illustrated and arrange three full roses on the top secured with royal icing. Assemble the tiers. Arrange the flower garlands so that one falls between each of the three roses on the top tier. Once the garlands are in position, place a fourth rose on top of the three to form a pyramid. Drape the garlands down the cake as shown. More bluebells can be pushed into the garlands and irises, bluebells and sweet peas added to the flower arrangement on the top tier. If you are using real flowers these should be added only at the last moment. The decoration is completed with sprigs of gypsophila and ribbon bows.

27 A completed garland should be long enough to stretch from the top of the cake to the bottom. Make the garlands fuller and thicker at the top and more delicate at the bottom.

CHRISTMAS TREE

Here is a simple and delicious orange madeira cake that proves it's possible to have your tree and eat it too! The tree (pictured on p. 135) is made from four 8″ (20cm) round cakes and the tub is a 6″ (15cm) cake. It requires only basic carving and shaping. The marzipanning and icing are deliberately left rough to create the illusion of branches and snow. Neither does the brushwork require a delicate hand. The finishing touches to the tree can be left to the children in the last busy days before Christmas.

To make the cake. Cream the butter or margarine and sugar together until light and fluffy. Add the eggs one at a time and beat into the mixture. Add a spoonful of flour to the mixture after each egg is incorporated and mix again. Sift the remaining flours together and fold into the creamed mixture, followed by the orange rind and juice. Turn the mixture into a greased and lined tin and level the top. Place in a preheated oven set at 160°C/325°F/Gas mark 3 for the time shown and cook until well risen and firm to the touch. Leave for 5–10 minutes then turn out on to a wire cooling rack.

INGREDIENTS

	6″ (15cm)	8″ (20cm)
butter or margarine	4oz (125g)	8oz (225g)
caster sugar	4oz (125g)	8oz (225g)
eggs	2	4
self-raising flour	4oz (125g)	8oz (225g)
plain flour	2oz (50g)	4oz (125g)
grated orange rind	1 orange	1½ oranges
approximate cooking time	1 hour	1 hour 25 minutes

Christmas Tree
Made from 4 × 8″ (20cm) and
1 × 6″ (15cm) orange madeira
cakes

Decoration
one 10″ (25cm) round cake
board
one 8″ (20cm) thin round cake
board
2lb (900g) marzipan
1lb (450g) royal icing
2lb (900g) fondant icing

apricot jam
dragees
small chocolates

Equipment
approx 1′ (30cm) of ¼″
dowelling
food colour
coloured foil
ribbon
candles and holders
heart-shaped cutter
star-shaped cutter

TIMESAVERS

TIMESAVER You can add green colouring to the fondant before rolling it out and icing the sections of the tree. The green will not be as deep as if you had painted it, but you can make up for this by decorating the tree with gaily coloured gifts.

TIMESAVER Icing the tree tub in 1″ (2.5cm) sections produces a traditional slatted look, but you could apply the icing in one piece. Turn the tub upside down and smooth over the icing. Cut off the excess. Turn the tub the right way up and score the slats into the icing with a cocktail stick.

TIMESAVER Instead of wrapping the presents, buy some colourful chocolate tree ornaments and stick them to the cake with royal icing. You could also use miniature Christmas tree decorations, as long as you remember which are edible and which are not.

DECORATION 4 hrs + drying time
Colouring the fondant icing saves 15 mins

ICING 1 hr 30 mins + 4 hrs drying time

COOKING 1 hr to 1 hr 25 mins per cake

MARZIPAN 1 hr 10 mins

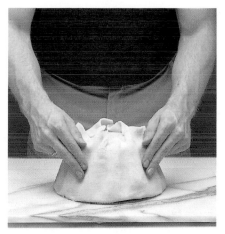

1 Assemble the four 8″ (20cm) madeira cakes on the thin 8″ (20cm) cake board. These cakes will form the carved branches of the tree and the board will eventually be placed on the tub.

3 Marzipan the three sections of the tree individually. For the lower third take 1lb (450g) marzipan. Spread the sides of the cake with apricot jam. Roll out the marzipan in a piece wide enough to reach from top to bottom of the cake and long enough to stretch round it. The measurements need not be precise as in other cakes. As you will see from the photograph it is not necessary to produce a completely flat finish, in fact the creases that form in the marzipan can be accentuated to produce the irregular effect of branches. Continue with the middle and top layers using 8oz (225g) and 4oz (125g) marzipan respectively. Trim off any excess marzipan.

2 To carve the cakes into the tree shape as illustrated, it may be helpful to separate the cakes, and then reassemble them to check for symmetry. The bottom two cakes represent the lower third of the tree, and the other two represent the middle and top sections. If you wish to add further detail at this stage, you could carve irregular ridges running from top to bottom in each section of the cake to represent branches, though this is not essential. To make the tub, take the 6″ (15cm) cake and carve to produce gently sloping sides as illustrated.

4 Take 12oz (350g) fondant icing and on a work surface lightly dusted with cornflour roll out a circle large enough to cover the top and sides of the bottom third of the cake. Drape it over the cake.

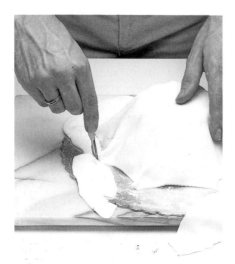

5 Once again, do not try to get rid of the creases, but emphasize them to add to the branch detail. Trim off the excess icing and repeat the process with the middle and top sections using 8oz (225g) and 6oz (175g) fondant icing respectively. Be sure to keep any fondant trimmings and wrap them in cling film as they will be needed to make the decorations for the tree. Allow the icing to dry for 4 hours before proceeding.

6 To ice the tub, spread the top and sides of the cake with apricot jam. Roll out the remaining marzipan with any trimmings that may have been left over. Use the 6″ (15cm) tin in which the cake was baked to cut a circle of marzipan and apply it to the top of the tub. With the remaining marzipan, make a strip long enough to go around the tub and wide enough to cover the sides. Fix to the sides of the tub. Measure and cut 4 pieces of dowelling to the height of the marzipanned tub. Insert into the cake as shown so that they are flush with the surface. This will give extra support to the tree.

TIPS

The tricky part with this cake is placing the fully decorated tree top on the small tub. If you want to avoid using the dowelling supports, you could replace the tub with a decorated plant pot. To prevent the pot tipping over, line it with a polythene bag and fill with flour or rice, which you will be able to use afterwards.

7 Take 4oz (125g) fondant icing and colour it Christmas red. The tub can be iced in one sheet or in strips 1″ (2.5cm) wide to represent wooden slats. Use a cocktail stick or skewer to score lines into the icing to produce or emphasize this effect.

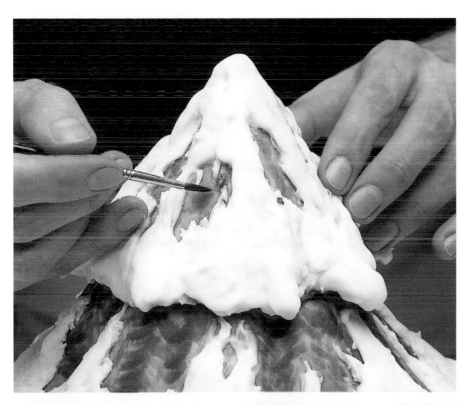

8 Now make up some green food colour and brush over the icing on the tree. The painting need not be completely even. Paint a herringbone pattern in a darker green on top to emphasize the branches. Leave to dry.

9 Take the royal icing and apply roughly to the cake as illustrated. Using either a paintbrush dipped in water or a wetted knife, gently smooth the icing to produce the rounded effect of a fresh and heavy fall of snow. Save a little icing to fix the decorations.

10 Take the chocolates and rewrap them in various coloured foils. Tie each parcel with a bow of narrow ribbon.

11 Take the candle holders and insert into the snow-laden boughs. Fix in the candles.

13 To make the other decorations take the icing trimmings from the tub and roll out again. Using a small heart-shaped cutter, cut out as many hearts as possible and allow to dry on greaseproof paper or non-stick cooking parchment. When dry, fix dragees in the centre of each heart with a dab of royal icing and fix to the tree. Another decoration that children can help make involves using the remaining 2oz (50g) fondant icing. Colour half the icing and leave the other half white. Roll out both pieces of icing. Cut an equal sized strip from both pieces, making it as wide as possible. Brush the surface of one piece with water and place the other piece on top. Once again brush the surface of the top piece with water and roll up the icing as in a Swiss roll. Cut the roll into thin slices and gently flatten with a rolling pin. This will produce an attractive spiral pattern. Using a small star-shaped cutter, cut out a star from the centre of each piece and allow to dry on greaseproof paper or non-stick parchment. When dry fix to the cake with a dab of royal icing.

12 Using a dab of royal icing fix the parcels to the tree.

ASSEMBLY

Paint two silver lines around the tub to look like metal hoops. Place the tree on its board on top of the tub. Serve at the table with the candles lit, and have a very Merry Christmas.

SUNDAY TEA CAKE

This Sunday tea cake, made with two airy Genoese sponges sandwiched with strawberries and cream (pictured on p. 139), is decorated colourfully and quickly without being iced. Instead, simply made red marzipan strawberries, each with a realistic green calyx, and green marzipan leaves are arranged attractively on the sugar-dusted top of the cake to complete this luxurious tea-time feast.

To make the cake. Line the bottom and sides of the tin with greaseproof paper. Brush the lining paper with butter and sprinkle the tin with flour. Tip out the excess flour. Sift the plain flour and salt together two or three times. If using butter, clarify by melting and skim off any froth. Pour the melted butter out of the pan leaving the milky sediment behind. Put the eggs in a large bowl, copper if possible, and add the sugar. Place the bowl in or over hot but not boiling water. Whisk for about 10 minutes until the mixture is thick enough to leave a trail when the whisk is lifted out of it. Take the bowl from the heat and continue beating until cool. Sift the flour and salt on to the mixture in three batches, folding in each batch as lightly as possible. If using the butter, add after the last batch of flour and fold in. Be careful to fold the butter in as lightly and quickly as possible as the mixture loses volume once the butter is added. Pour the mixture into the prepared tin and bake in a preheated oven set at 180°C/350°F/Gas mark 4 for about 35–40 minutes until the cake shrinks slightly from the sides of the tin and the top springs back when lightly pressed.

INGREDIENTS

Cake (for one sponge)
4 eggs
4oz (125g) sugar
4oz (125g) plain flour
pinch of salt
2oz (50g) butter (optional)

Filling and decoration
½ pint (284ml) double or whipping cream
strawberries
1¼lb (575g) white marzipan
icing sugar to dust
a little royal icing

Equipment
food colour
piping bag with ½″ (1cm) star nozzle
star-shaped cutter

TIMESAVERS

TIMESAVER Save time and money by making only one sponge and splitting it in half before decorating the top.

TIMESAVER If you have your own strawberry patch, you could use real strawberries and leaves to decorate the cake, extending the decoration on to the cake stand or plate.

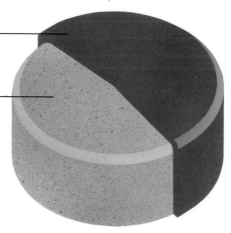

DECORATION 1 hr 30 mins
Up to 1 hour can be saved by using real strawberries for decoration

COOKING 40 mins per cake

1 Take the two cakes and brush away any loose crumbs from the sides.

2 Whip the cream into soft peaks. Spread half the cream on the surface of one of the cakes and put the other half into a piping bag fitted with a ½″ (1cm) star nozzle. Pipe swirls of cream all around the edge of the cake.

3 Slice the strawberries in half and place some between the swirls of cream on the edge. Pile the remaining strawberries cut edge down in the centre of the cake.

4 Place the second cake on top of the fruit and dust the surface lightly with icing sugar.

5 Take 12oz (350g) of the marzipan and colour it red with edible food colour. Cut the marzipan into 1oz (25g) pieces and roll into strawberry shapes. Using a cocktail stick or skewer, prick the marzipan strawberries at intervals all over the surface.

6 Colour the remaining 8oz (225g) of marzipan green. On a work surface lightly dusted with cornflour, roll out the marzipan. Using a star-shaped cutter, press out a calyx for each strawberry. Press a skewer or the end of a paintbrush into the centre of the calyx to draw up the points. Fix the calyx to the strawberry with a little royal icing. Gather up the remaining marzipan and roll out. Cut out several leaves and score veins on them with a cocktail stick. With the marzipan left, roll out four long thin strands about the thickness of a drinking straw. Cut one of them into ¼" (5mm) lengths. Take each of these small pieces and roll one end into a point. Fix to the centre of the calyx on the strawberry with a little royal icing. Take the remaining lengths of marzipan and arrange on the cake.

ASSEMBLY

Place the strawberries and leaves on top of the cake, taking care not to disturb the icing sugar.

'WINNERS'

The technique of icing marquetry featured here – making pictures with shapes of different coloured icing – can be used to create any bold design and is particularly effective in the portrayal of cartoon characters. The Union Jack with its torch and laurel wreath (p.143) can mark the occasion of any victory from an Olympic medal downwards. The flag itself could be replaced with a club badge or colours. The basic cake is made from two 12" (30cm) square coconut and cherry cakes piled on top of one another.

To make the cake. Grease and line a tin with greaseproof paper. Mix the butter or margarine with the sugar and beat until light and fluffy. Add the eggs one at a time, followed by a spoonful of flour. Fold in the remaining flour and the salt alternating with some of the milk. Add the salt. Mix the cherries with the coconut and fold into the mixture. Turn the mixture into the tin and bake in a preheated oven set at 180°C/350°F/Gas mark 4 for about 50 minutes until firm to the touch. Turn out on to a wire rack to cool.

Although there is no filling in this cake, you might like to fill it with a cherry, coconut and vanilla cream, made as follows. Take 8oz (225g) butter or margarine and mix in 1lb (450g) icing sugar. Fold in 4oz (125g) finely chopped glacé cherries and 2oz (50g) desiccated coconut. Use to sandwich the two cakes together.

INGREDIENTS

(for one cake)
9oz (250g) butter or margarine
8oz (225g) caster sugar
4oz (125g) soft dark brown sugar
3 eggs
12oz (350g) self-raising flour
¾ teaspoon salt
9 fl oz (270ml) milk
8oz (225g) glacé cherries, quartered
4oz (125g) desiccated coconut

Decoration
14" (35cm) square cake board
1lb (450g) white fondant icing
8oz (225g) red fondant icing
12oz (350g) blue fondant icing
1lb (450g) gelatin icing
1½lb (675g) marzipan
apricot jam

Equipment
12" (30cm) of thick wire, such as a wire coathanger
modelling wire for leaves and flames
gutteroll florists' tape

TIMESAVERS

TIMESAVER If you have decided not to bother cutting an undulating surface to the top of your cake, you will find that you also save time on the decoration. If you decorate the top of the cake alone, wrap the side of the cake in a broad red, white and blue ribbon to complete the decoration.

TIMESAVER You could use real leaves in the laurel crown instead of making them from icing. If you don't have a laurel bush in your garden, ivy leaves would look just as good, and as they are hardy they would keep fresh even if the decoration was made the day before.

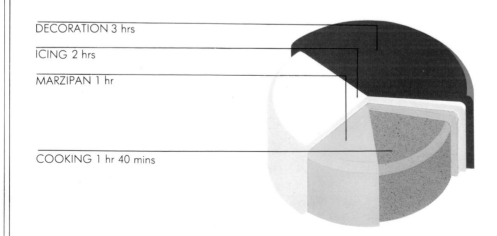

DECORATION 3 hrs

ICING 2 hrs

MARZIPAN 1 hr

COOKING 1 hr 40 mins

1 Cut the cakes into oblongs 12 × 9" (30 × 23cm). Put the cakes on top of one another and trim the top to make a regular block of cake. Using a kitchen knife carefully cut an undulating surface into the cake as shown.

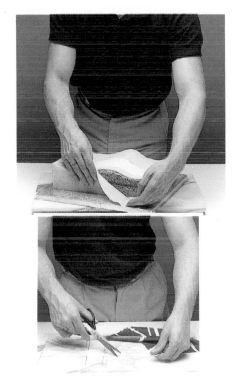

2 Take a piece of greaseproof paper and lay on the surface of the cake. Trace the outline of the cake. Take more greaseproof paper and trace the shape of the four sides of the cake. These templates will be used in cutting out the marzipan. Spread the surface of the cake with apricot jam. On a work surface lightly dusted with icing sugar roll out 12oz (350g) of the marzipan into a sheet large enough to contain the template for the top. Lay the greaseproof outline on the marzipan and cut round it. Fix the marzipan on top of the cake. Roll out the remaining marzipan and cut out the pieces for the sides of the cake using the templates. Fix them to the cake. Let the marzipan dry for two hours before proceeding, copy the design on to a piece of greaseproof or tracing paper. With blue and red crayons or food colour pens, mark out the sections of the design in appropriate colours. Cut out the blue and red sections. Note that the size of the template will vary according to whether or not you intend to continue the flag pattern down the sides of the cake.

3 On a work surface lightly dusted with cornflour roll out 1lb (450g) of white fondant icing into a sheet large enough to cover the cake. Drape the icing over the cake and smooth over the sides and down the corners. Using a sharp knife trim the icing along the edges of the cake and use scissors to trim the corners. Roll out the red icing and lay the template for the large red cross on top. Cut out the cross and lay in position on

the cake. Gather up the red icing remains and roll out again. Take the templates for the smaller red cross running diagonally across the flag and cut out the four pieces. Lay in position on the cake. Take the blue fondant icing and roll out. Cut out the eight blue pieces with the aid of the templates and lay on the cake. Trim the icing to the edge of the cake with a sharp knife, shaping it to continue down the sides.

4 Take 8oz (225g) gelatin icing and divide into balls the size of hazelnuts. Cut the modelling wire into 3" (7.5cm) lengths and insert into the icing balls. Roll out each piece so that the wire extends well inside it. Using a sharp knife cut out leaves and score veins into them with a cocktail stick. Allow the leaves to dry flat for about 4 hours. Paint green and allow to dry again.

5 Take the coathanger wire and bend into a horseshoe shape. Wrap gutteroll florists' tape around it. Place the leaves on the wire as you go and secure by wrapping the gutteroll over the wire stalks of the leaves.

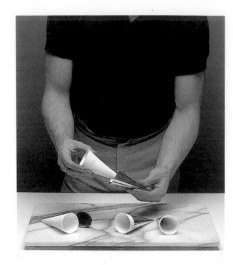

6 To make the cone for the torch, take any mould that is cone-shaped. In this instance a

cream horn mould was used, but you could make a mould from stiff card. Wrap the cone in grease-proof paper, cut to the shape of the cone and secure with sticky tape. Cut down one side and open out to form a template. Roll out 4oz (125g) gelatin icing and lay the template on top. Cut round the paper template. Take the icing piece and carefully make into a cone. Place the icing cone inside the cone mould to dry for at least 4 hours. The flames for the torch are made like the leaves for the crown described in step 5. The flames are irregular in shape as illustrated and are cut from the remaining 4oz (125g) gelatin icing. Allow the flames to dry flat.

9 Fill the cone with tissue or kitchen paper, or a piece of florists' oasis, and insert the wire to fix the flames in position. Take all the flames and fix together.

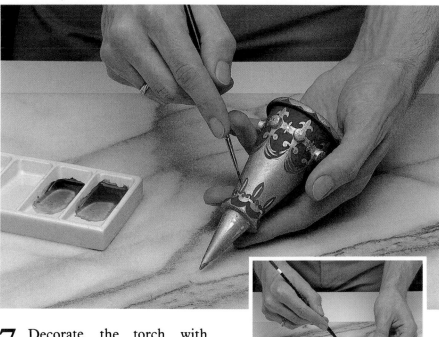

7 Decorate the torch with food colours of your choice. This particular design is quite complex and has been further embellished by the addition of strips of icing around the top edge of the cone and again about two thirds down its length. There are also small cut-out circles of icing studded around the top of the cone. It is not necessary for the cone to be quite so highly decorated, and the use of gold and silver with possibly one other colour could be just as effective.

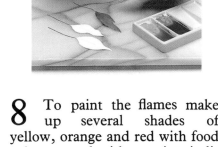

8 To paint the flames make up several shades of yellow, orange and red with food colours, and either paint individual flames in separate colours or use all the colours on each flame.

10 An alternative and easier way of making the cone would be to buy an ice cream cone and paint it gold with food colour. The flames could then be made from red tissue paper.

ASSEMBLY

Place the torch in the centre of the cake and fix in position with a little royal icing. Place the laurel crown so that it frames the torch in the centre of the cake.

PARTRIDGE IN A PEAR TREE

A partridge in a pear tree may be a traditional Christmas image, but there is nothing traditional about the decoration of the cake pictured on p.147, or indeed about the cake itself, which is two whisky cakes sandwiched together with lemon and honey filling. The bird, fruit and leaves are cut from different thicknesses of marzipan and applied underneath the fondant, giving a three-dimensional effect to the decoration. The deep midnight blue background is a bold move away from the traditional red, green and gold of Christmas time.

To make the cake. Grease and line a 10″ (25cm) round cake tin with greaseproof paper. Cream the butter and sugar until light and fluffy. Gradually beat in the finely grated rind of half the lemon and the eggs. Fold in half the sifted flour and then add the whisky. Fold in the remaining flour. Spoon into the prepared tin and bake in a preheated oven at 160°C/325°F/Gas mark 3 for about 50 minutes to one hour. Check the cake after about 40 or 45 minutes. If it is getting too brown, cover with a sheet of newspaper or kitchen foil. The cake is ready when firm to the touch. Remove from the tin and allow to cool.

For the filling, cream the softened butter or margarine with the sugar. Add the honey. If a firmer filling is required, add more icing sugar. Add the lemon juice and mix together.

INGREDIENTS

Cake
6oz (175g) butter or margarine
6oz (175g) soft brown sugar
1 lemon
3 eggs, beaten
6oz (175g) sifted self-raising flour
4 tablespoons (60ml) whisky

Filling
4oz (125g) butter or margarine
8oz (225g) sifted icing sugar
4oz (125g) runny honey
1–2 tablespoons (15–30ml) lemon juice

Decoration
12″ (30cm) round cake board
4½lb (2kg) marzipan
2lb (900g) fondant icing
apricot jam
royal icing

Equipment
food colours
pieces of *diamanté*

TIMESAVERS

TIMESAVER Most of the time spent decorating this cake is devoted to moulding the marzipan shapes before icing. You can save a lot of time by moulding decoration for the top only.

TIMESAVER To simplify the decoration on the top of the cake concentrate on cutting out just the partridge and the pears in marzipan. Place these in position as described and then ice over. Make the leaves separately as in the box of roses (p.64)

and fix to the cake with royal icing once the bird and the pears have been painted. You could either use real ribbon or cut thin strips of red fondant icing and drape them over the decoration.

TIMESAVER The midnight blue colouring around the decoration can be left out if you wish. If you decide to leave the icing white, add a ribbon round the side of the cake to introduce depth of colour into your design.

DECORATION 3 hrs + 5 hrs drying time for food colour

ICING 30 mins + 8 hrs drying time

MARZIPAN 1 hr 30 mins + 4 hrs drying time

COOKING 1 hr per cake.

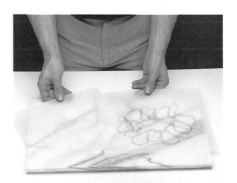

1 The design for the top of this cake can be found on *p.186*. It is a good idea to trace it out twice – use one tracing to position the elements in the design and the other to cut out the pieces of marzipan. Trace the design for the side of the cake.

2 Sandwich the cakes together with the filling.

3 On a work surface lightly dusted with icing sugar roll out 12oz (350g) marzipan. Using the tin in which the cake was baked as a guide, cut out a circle to fit the top of the cake. Spread the top of the cake with apricot jam and fix on the circle. Wrap a piece of string round the cake to measure its circumference, and measure its height. Roll out a further 12oz (350g) marzipan into a strip and cut to the measurements just noted. To make it easier to handle, cut in half. Spread the side of the cake with apricot jam and fix the marzipan to it. Allow to dry for a couple of hours.

4 To decorate the top of the cake, roll out 6oz (175g) marzipan fairly thinly. Place one tracing over the marzipan and cut out the leaves as shown. Place these in position on top of the cake using the other tracing as a guide and fix to the first layer of marzipan with a little apricot jam. Roll out a further 6oz (175g) marzipan into a slightly thicker layer. Cut out the partridge and fix on the cake with apricot jam. Roll out 12oz (350g) marzipan into a still thicker layer and cut out the pears. Round down the edges. Place the pears in position and fix to the cake with jam. To decorate the side of the cake roll out 12oz (350g) marzipan into a strip long enough to stretch half way round the cake and wide enough to contain the decoration on your tracing. Making sure that the tracing will also stretch half way round the cake, lay it on the marzipan and cut out the design. Fix to the side of the cake with jam. Use only

enough jam to make the marzipan stick – too much and the weight of the marzipan will cause it to slip down the side of the cake. Repeat for the other half of the cake. If you would like to add more relief decoration to the side of the cake, cut out more pear shapes from any leftover marzipan and fix in place with jam. Allow to dry for two hours.

5 On a work surface lightly dusted with cornflour roll out the fondant icing into a sheet large enough to cover the cake. Moisten the side of the cake with water to make it sticky and lay the icing over the cake. Using a flat-bladed knife held against the side trim off any excess icing. With fingers lightly coated in cornflour gently mould the icing into the marzipan detail on the top and side of the cake. Allow to dry for eight hours or overnight.

7 To paint the pears, make up a series of yellow, pale green and red food colours. Apply them one after the other while still wet and mix with the brush to create a delicate shaded effect. Leave to dry for an hour.

Paint the ribbon decoration in deep Christmas red food colour. Leave to dry for an hour.

8 To paint the leaves, make up two or three shades of green and apply one after the other, mixing with the brush while still wet. Use a darker shade of green to paint the veins on the leaves. Leave to dry for an hour.

6 To paint the partridge make up a series of brown, red and orange-brown food colours. The bird's markings have been stylized in order to make colouring simpler. Transfer these to the icing from your tracing with a cocktail stick. Start by outlining the markings with unbroken lines of dark brown. Allow to dry for 20 minutes or so, then continue by filling in the various sections in different shades as shown.

Add gold highlights on the feathers for further effect. Leave to dry for an hour before proceeding.

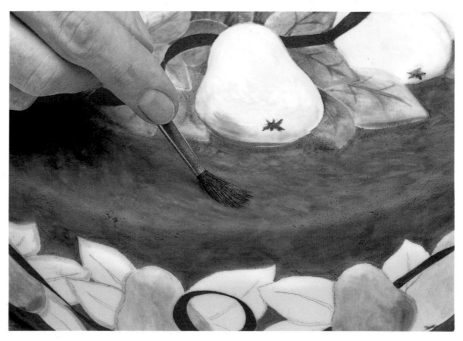

9 To colour the background, make up a rich midnight blue and brush on to the un-coloured icing. Do not worry that you will see the brushstrokes – that the cake is hand-painted is a great part of its charm. Paint on the colour with the bristles splayed out to emphasize this. Gently press the tip of the brush all over the blue icing to produce a stippled effect.

FIRST NIGHT

The First Night cake (pictured on p.153) is a wholesome 10" (25 cm) fruit cake and its decoration features careful hand painting to create a striking illusion of perspective, and moulded masks of gelatin icing. You can buy masks to take moulds from or make simpler versions with cut-out features. The masks could be decorated to represent specific characters – here they are embellished with gold leaf. The pillar is moulded on a candlestick in two halves, which are then stuck together with royal icing. The dramatic red curtain is made of tragacanth icing.

To make the cake. Mix together the dried fruit, glacé cherries, spices and ground almonds. Cream the butter or margarine until soft, then add the sugar and beat until light and fluffy. Do not overbeat. Add the eggs one at a time, beating well, followed by a spoonful of flour. Fold in the remaining flour, followed by the dried fruit mixture. Add the honey and lemon rind. Grease and double line a 10" (23cm) square cake tin with greaseproof paper. Level the surface of the cake. Tie two or three thicknesses of brown paper or newspaper around the tin. Bake in a preheated oven at 150°C/300°F/Gas mark 2 for four hours 15 minutes or until cooked. To prevent the cake from burning on top, cover with a double thickness of brown paper or newspaper after half the cooking time. Test with a cocktail stick to see if the cake is ready. If the cake is done, the stick will come out clean. Leave to cool in the tin, then turn out.

TIMESAVERS

TIMESAVER The picture frame effect created by the marzipanning of the sides of the cake allows for the continuation of the black and white theme.

An alternative way of decorating the sides would be to drape red fondant icing all the way around the cake like a theatre curtain.

DECORATION 4 hrs and a total of 12 hrs drying time

ICING 45 mins + 8 hrs drying time

MARZIPAN 1 hr 30 mins + 6 hrs drying time

COOKING 4 hrs 15 mins

INGREDIENTS

Cake
1lb 2oz (500g) currants
13oz (375g) sultanas
13oz (375g) raisins
8oz (225g) glacé cherries
2 teaspoons cinnamon
1½ teaspoons mixed spice
5oz (150g) ground almonds
1lb 2oz (500g) butter or margarine
1lb 2oz (500g) soft brown sugar
9 eggs
1lb 5oz (600g) plain wholemeal flour
2 tablespoons honey
grated rind of 1 lemon

Decoration
12" (30cm) square cake board
4½lb (2kg) marzipan
2lb (900g) fondant icing
1lb (450g) Christmas red tragacanth or gelatin icing
2¼lb (1kg) gelatin icing, uncoloured
royal icing
apricot jam

Equipment
dowelling
food colours
baby ribbon
gold leaf
water gold size
moulds for masks

1 Prepare the cake for marzipanning as in the instructions for the Three-tiered Wedding Cake on *p.121*. Turn the cake upside down on the board. Roll 1lb (450g) marzipan into a long sausage on a work surface lightly dusted with icing sugar. Gently press it into the gap between the cake and the board all round the cake. Hold a flat-bladed knife against the side of the cake and cut off any excess marzipan. Spread

the top of the cake with apricot jam. Roll out 1½lb (675g) marzipan and cut out a circle to fit the top using the tin in which the cake was baked as a guide. Fix in position on top of the cake. Measure the depth of the cake. Roll out 12oz (350g) marzipan and cut out two rectangles measuring 10″ (25cm) long by the depth of the cake. Spread opposite sides of the cake with apricot jam and fix the marzipan in position. Measure the length of the other two sides to take into account the depth of the marzipan just applied. Cut out two rectangles to fit from a further 12oz (350g) marzipan, spread the cake with apricot jam and fix the marzipan in position. Carefully smooth the top and sides of the cake with a plastic sheet to ensure that all surfaces are flat and the seams are as neat as possible. Leave to dry for four hours.

2 Roll out 8oz (225g) marzipan and cut out eight strips measuring ½″ (1cm) wide by the length of the sides of the cake. Spread the strips with a little jam and fix to the top and bottom edges of the cake. Do not use too much jam or the weight of the marzipan may cause the top strips to slip down the sides of the cake. When in position take a sharp knife and trim the ends of each strip to an angle of 45°. Take up the marzipan remains and roll out another eight strips ½″ (1cm) wide and to the depth of the cake. Trim the top and bottom of each strip to an angle of 45°. Spread the strips sparingly with apricot jam and fix to the corners so that the angled pieces fit neatly together as shown. The effect created is that of a picture frame on each side of the cake. Allow to dry for two hours.

TIPS

It is particularly important to have a flawlessly smooth finish to this cake. One of the purposes of moistening the marzipan before icing is to ensure against trapping air bubbles between the two layers. Instead of water you could use any alcoholic spirit for this purpose to give a little additional flavour.

4 Masks to use as moulds can be bought in department stores, or you could use the face of a large doll. You could even cut out a simple mask shape and let it dry over a large tin of beans. Once the icing has dried you can cut details of eyes and mouth in a smile and a grimace to represent comedy and tragedy. In this case, bought masks have been used as moulds and each has been covered with 6oz (175g) gelatin icing. On a work surface lightly dusted with cornflour roll out the gelatin icing and lay over the mask. Gently press the icing into the detail. Cut around the mask with a sharp knife to trim off excess icing. Leave to dry for at least four hours.

3 Moisten the sides of the cake with a little water to make the marzipan sticky. On a work surface lightly dusted with cornflour roll out 2lb (900g) fondant icing into a sheet large enough to cover the cake. Place the icing sheet on the cake and gently smooth into the detail on the sides. Press the icing into neat seams at the corners and trim off the excess with sharp scissors. Hold a flat-bladed knife against the side of the cake and trim off any excess icing. Make the seams as neat as possible, smoothing the icing to mould the pieces around the corners into one piece. Allow the icing to dry for eight hours or overnight.

Trace the design for the top of the cake from *p.187* on to a piece of greaseproof paper. Enlarge the pattern to fit the size of your particular cake. Lay the pattern on top of the cake and secure with small pins. Be sure to remember exactly how many pins you have used. Using a ruler and cocktail stick gently score along the lines of the pattern so as to leave a faint trace of the design on the surface of the icing. Be careful not to move the pattern. When you have finished, remove the pins and pattern and draw over the scored lines with a black food colour pen against a ruler. Be careful not to smudge the colour by dragging the ruler across it. It is a good idea to draw all the lines in one direction, then wait for 10 minutes or so until they have dried before drawing the second set of lines. Take care too not to smudge the colour Take a medium paintbrush and black food colour and following your pattern paint alternating squares black. Allow the colour to dry for four hours.

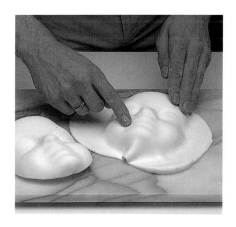

5 We have chosen to use genuine English gold leaf to embellish the masks. The effect is quite stunning and the gold leaf is easy to use. Each piece measures 3″ (7.5cm) square and is stuck on a fine tissue backing. To transfer the gold to the mask, first paint the mask with water gold size, which will leave it tacky. Place the gold leaf on the tacky surface and gently smooth it down. Pull back the fine tissue, leaving the gold on the mask. Although ordinary gold

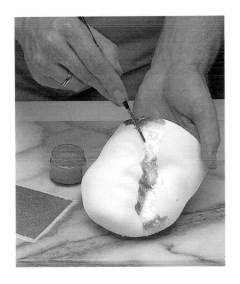

leaf is edible, the type requiring the use of size is not, so the masks will be purely decorative. As it is not always possible to produce a perfect covering on a curved surface we have added finger gold (used on picture frames) of various shades for an antique effect. Even on the partly decorated mask we have deliberately left the surface looking 'distressed'. Other ways of decorating the masks are with food colours, poster paints, sequins, feathers, fabric, ribbons or jewellery.

When the masks are completed stick a short piece of dowelling to the back of the mask with stiff royal icing or glue. The length of dowelling will depend on how high you want the mask to stand above the cake. Here the prop for one mask is 12″ (30cm) and for the other 9″ (23cm).

6 On a work surface lightly dusted with cornflour roll out 12oz (350g) gelatin icing and cut out four rectangles 1½″ × 8½″ (4 × 21cm). Allow to dry for four hours, turning the pieces over at least once. The design for the decorative panelling can be found on *p.187*. Trace the design on to greaseproof paper and enlarge it if necessary to fit your cake. Lay a piece of graphite paper on top of the panel and place the tracing over it. Transfer the design on to the icing and draw over it with black food colour pen. Leave to dry for 10 minutes. Make up black and grey food colours (grey is just watered-down black) and paint the panels as illustrated. Leave to dry for an hour. The small grey geometrics can be further decorated with delicate black lines to produce a marbled effect. When dry fix the panelling to the sides of the cake in the 'picture frames' with a little royal icing.

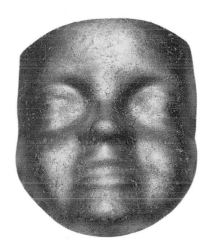

7 The column is modelled on a 9″ (23cm) candlestick. If you do not have a suitable candlestick, you could use the centre of a roll of kitchen paper to make a simplified column.

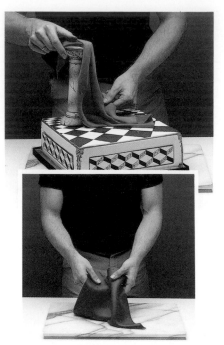

8 On a work surface lightly dusted with cornflour roll out 6oz (175g) gelatin icing and lay over the candlestick. Gently smooth the icing into the detail. Using a sharp knife, trim away the excess icing from the sides and top, leaving a neat edge at the half-way line. Let the half-iced column dry for several hours or overnight if possible. Repeat the process to make a second half-column and when completely dry stick the two halves together with royal icing. Allow the completed column to dry for four hours.

11 Fix the column securely in position on top of the cake with stiff royal icing. Allow to dry for an hour. The curtain is made of tragacanth icing – it sets hard when dry but is remarkably elastic while it is being moulded. At a pinch gelatin icing could be used, but this dries out quickly and so might not fold and drape as easily. On a work surface lightly dusted with cornflour, roll out the traga-canth icing as thinly as possible into a 12″ (30cm) square. Drape it carefully over the column, using royal icing to help stick it to the top. Arrange the curtain decorat-ively on the surface of the cake. Take care that the weight of the curtain is supported by the cake as well as by the column, or it could split and tear. Once the curtain is safely in position, allow to dry overnight.

9 To decorate the column make up some fairly thick black food colour. Take a tooth-brush and dip the bristles into the colour. Hold the toothbrush as shown and draw your thumb briskly over the bristles to flick a fine mist of colour on to the column. The colour needs to be quite thick to prevent it dripping down the column.

10 With a fine paintbrush, paint a delicate tracing of lines on the column and add dec-orative lines and swirls at the top and bottom. If you wish, gold highlights could be added too.

ASSEMBLY

Carefully push the dowelling supports on the back of the masks into the sur-face of the cake and right down to the board. Tie a piece of white baby ribbon round the edge of the cake and secure with a dab of royal icing.

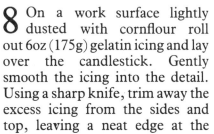

THE TEDDY BEARS' PICNIC

The full range of minute detail can be included in this project when time and patience allow. However, the cake can be simplified in a number of ways without losing the sense of fun. Anyone who receives this cake will have the pleasure of a permanent reminder of the thought you put into it in the shape of a ready-made teddy bears' party to keep.

Cream the butter and sugar together until light and fluffy. Beat in the eggs, one at a time, then a tablespoon of flour. Sift the rest of the flour on to the creamed mixture and fold in using a metal spoon. Fold in the lemon juice. Turn the mixture into a 9″ (25 cm) round greased and lined tin. Bake in a preheated oven at 160°C/325°F/Gas mark 3 for 1½ hours. Cool in the tin for 5 minutes before turning out on to a wire rack. When it is completely cool remove lining paper.

Slit the cake in half; cover the bottom half with the curd cheese, then with the conserve. Place the top half back in position.

TIMESAVERS

TIMESAVER The decoration in this particular cake includes all surfaces of the cake and board. To save time it is possible to restrict decoration to the top of the cake. Marzipan and ice the cake as for the three-tiered wedding cake on page 82 and wrap a colourful ribbon round the side.

TIMESAVER Several items on the cake can be replaced with non-edible alternatives. For example, instead of making miniature water lilies, small dried flowerheads can be used, or instead of an umbrella made of icing, a paper cocktail parasol could be included.

TIMESAVER Although the teddy bears are very much a central feature of this cake, it is possible to cut down on the time required to make them. Yellow marzipan is an ideal material in which to mould the bears and they look very good without the addition of swimming costumes and strawhats. In fact by simply decorating the face with black dots for eyes and nose you can make the resulting character just as lovable.

INGREDIENTS

Cake
10 oz (300 g) butter
10 oz (300 g) caster sugar
5 eggs (size 1 or 2)
10 oz (300 g) self-raising flour
5 oz (150 g) plain flour
2 tablespoons lemon juice

Filling
12 oz (350 g) curd cheese,
sweetened to taste
with caster sugar
12 oz (350 g) black cherry
conserve or jam of your choice

Decoration
14″ (35 cm) round cake board
2½ lb (1125 g) marzipan,
1 lb (450 g) for the cake
4 oz (125 g) conserve or jam,
2 lb (900 g) fondant icing
12 oz (350 g) gelatin icing,
small amount of royal icing

Equipment
food colours
musical movement (optional)

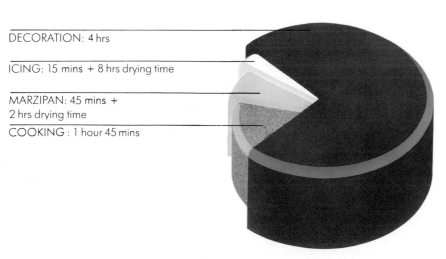

DECORATION: 4 hrs

ICING: 15 mins + 8 hrs drying time

MARZIPAN: 45 mins +
2 hrs drying time

COOKING : 1 hour 45 mins

1 Using a sharp knife, cut a series of steps into the surface and side of the cake to form the waterfall.

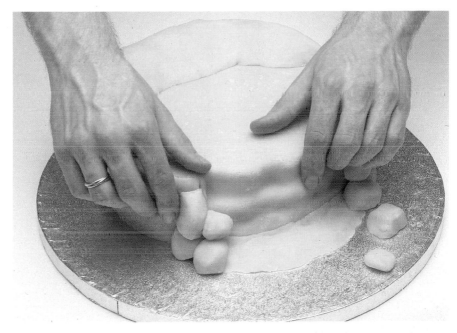

2 Spread the top surface of the cake and the waterfall with a thin layer of jam. Roll out 8 oz (225 g) of the marzipan and place on the surface prepared with jam. Mould the marzipan into the steps. Trim the marzipan round the top edge of the cake and the sides of the waterfall. Using a further 8 oz (225 g) of marzipan, cut out a strip to the depth of the cake and place around the side, having first spread the sides of the cake with a thin layer of jam.

TIP BOX

Not everyone is fond of marzipan and it can certainly be rather costly. In order not to waste any of the cake and at the same time cut down on the amount of marzipan used, cut up the cake left after carving the waterfall in step 1 and chop it roughly into blocks. Fix these on to the sides of the cake before marzipanning, using a little jam from the filling, and proceed with step 2, wrapping marzipan over the blocks.

3 Take 6 oz (175 g) of marzipan and mould in a rough crescent shape to form the grassy bank at the back of the cake; spread a little jam on the underside of the marzipan and fix to the surface of the cake. Take 2 oz (50 g) of marzipan and press on to the board to form the bottom of the waterfall. Take 4 oz (125 g) of marzipan and mould into irregular blocks to form the rocks at the side of the waterfall. Fix to the cake with a small amount of jam.

4 Roll out the fondant icing and cover the cake and board. With hands dusted with cornflour, gently mould the icing to the shape of the cake, emphasizing the details. Trim surplus icing to the edge of the board.

5 Using food colours and paste, mix up a number of shades of blue, adding more water to produce a lighter colour. Take a medium-sized paint brush and, starting near the edge, dab the colour on to the icing to form the lily pond, with darker blue towards the centre to give the impression of depth. Using this same technique, apply the colour to the pool at the base of the waterfall. To achieve the effect of the waterfall, flatten out the bristles of the brush in the food colour, as illustrated, and brush lightly over the steps up the waterfall.

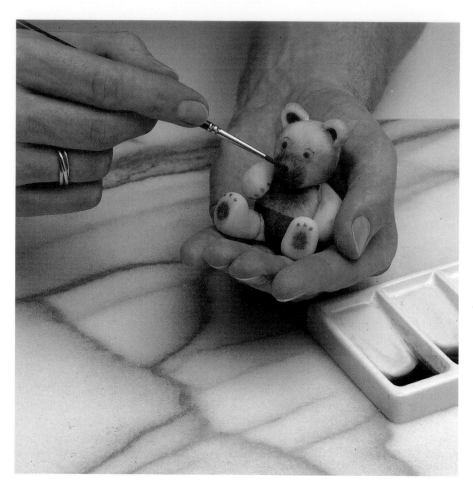

6 To create the grass effect on the bank and around the sides of the waterfall, brush the icing all over with a green food colour. While this is still wet, use a damp paint brush to dab the surface to produce a mottled effect. Paint the stones at the side of the waterfall with a mixture of green and brown food colours.

7 Using 4 oz (125 g) of marzipan for each bear, mould as illustrated. Fix the pieces together in various positions, using a little royal icing.

8 Take a small paint brush and a little brown food colour and paint the features on to the bears. Using one or more bright food colours, add the swimming costumes.

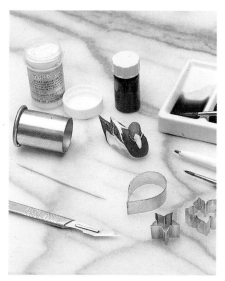

9 Take 4 oz (125 g) of gelatin icing and roll out into a thin sheet. Cut out various sized circles for the plates, cups and lily leaves using a biscuit cutter, or cut around various sizes of coins.

10 To make the straw boaters, once again cut out circles of icing, ensuring that the smaller circle is cut out of a slightly thicker layer of icing. To create the straw effect, while the icing is still damp press gently against the fine wire mesh of a sieve. Lay flat and allow to dry completely. Fix the two circles together, using a little royal icing. Paint and wrap around a short length of narrow ribbon.

11 To form plates, allow the circles of icing to dry in the bottom of a wine glass to produce a slight curve. When dry, paint on a decorative design. To form cups, allow the circles of icing to dry over a thimble. Paint when dry.

13 To make the umbrella, cut out a larger circle of icing, approximately 3″ (7.5 cm) in diameter as illustrated, and allow to dry on a curved surface, such as a ladle. Then paint in bright colours. Attach a thin wooden skewer or cocktail stick to the underside of the umbrella, using stiff royal icing, and leave to dry.

To make the picnic basket, cut out rectangles of icing. Use a large rectangle at the back to make the lid. Assemble the basket with a little royal icing; paint with food colour to get a straw effect.

To make the tablecloth, cut a square and allow to dry curved over the edge of a square box or cake tin. When dry, paint in a checked pattern with blue food colour.

Attach water lilies, umbrella, straw boaters etc. to the cake with a little royal icing.

12 To make the water lily leaves, cut a narrow wedge from the centre to the edge of a circle of icing, and leave to dry flat. Paint, using green food colour, brushing from the centre to the edge.

To make water lilies, take a small star-shaped flower cutter and press out three stars for each flower. Place one star on top of the other, fixing with a dab of water. Press gently in the centre of the flower, so the petals bend upwards. Allow to dry and paint the centres yellow.

TIPS

Working in miniature and in some detail – for example on the lilies, crockery and parasol – might seem a rather daunting task. A way round this could be to colour the icing before icing and do without the intricate brushwork patterns on the tea service. The parasol could be made from icing in which the colour has been incompletely mixed, producing an attractive marbled effect.

14 Take a small ball of gelatin icing and mould the ducks as illustrated. Score the sides of the duck with a cocktail stick to produce the impression of wings.

15 Paint as illustrated and attach to cake with a little royal icing.

16 Take a small amount of the remaining gelatin icing and mould fruit, food and bottles as illustrated. Paint with food colours and attach with royal icing.

SPECIAL FEATURE

As a special feature, a musical movement has been incorporated into the decoration of the cake in the form of a gramophone. Such musical movements are available in good toy or model shops. To make the gramophone speaker, roll out a thin sheet of gelatin icing and press gently into one of the sections of an egg carton.

Using the remaining gelatin icing, cut out the sides and top of the gramophone, which should be similar in size to a matchbox. Cut a small groove into one side of the box for the winding handle. Fix the box together with a little royal icing. Paint a wood effect with brown food colour. Add the detail of the turntable, record and record arm as illustrated. Using a sharp knife, cut around the top edge leaving a small lip. Allow to dry and paint. Fix on to the gramophone with a small amount of royal icing.

BODY BEAUTIFUL

A 12" (30cm) square carrot and fruit cake celebrates health and fitness in the form of the Body Beautiful, pictured on p. 165. achieving a three-dimensional effect without carving or sculpting. Once the first layer of marzipan has been applied to the cake, the muscles and swimming trunks are moulded from different thicknesses of marzipan and fixed in position before the cake is iced.

To make the cake. Mix the sugar, honey, carrots, raisins, dates, nutmeg, butter and water together in a saucepan. Bring to the boil and simmer for 5 minutes. Turn into a mixing bowl and leave to cool. Stir in the beaten eggs. Mix the flours and the baking powder together and sprinkle on to the mixture. Carefully fold in the flour.

Grease and line a 12" (30cm) square cake tin with greaseproof paper or cooking parchment. Grease the lined tin and sprinkle with flour. Remove excess flour. Turn the mixture into the prepared tin and bake in a preheated oven at 180°C/350°F/Gas mark 4 for an hour or until firm to the touch. Cool on a wire rack.

TIMESAVERS

TIMESAVER As an alternative to cutting the muscles out of marzipan as described, you could score them into the marzipan covering the cake. Knead it well before applying to make it warm, soft and therefore more pliable. Score the outlines of the muscles with the end of a paintbrush. When the fondant is applied it will settle into the lines and the muscles will become apparent.

TIMESAVER Replace the icing rosette with one that has been won by the recipient of the cake, or tie an extravagant bow at the hip in its place.

I N G R E D I E N T S

Cake
12oz (350g) soft brown sugar
1lb (450g) clear honey
1¼lb (575g) finely grated carrot
12oz (350g) raisins
8oz (225g) chopped dates
2½ teaspoons ground nutmeg
12oz (350g) butter
¾ pint (450ml) water
3 eggs, beaten
12oz (350g) wholemeal flour
12oz (350g) plain flour, sifted
6 teaspoons baking powder, sifted

Decoration
16" (40cm) square cake board
2lb (900g) marzipan
2lb (900g) fondant icing, 1½lb (675g) flesh coloured for the body, 6oz (175g) yellow for the trunks and 2oz (50g) deeper flesh coloured for the nipples
apricot jam
royal icing

Equipment
ribbon for the edge and across the top of the cake

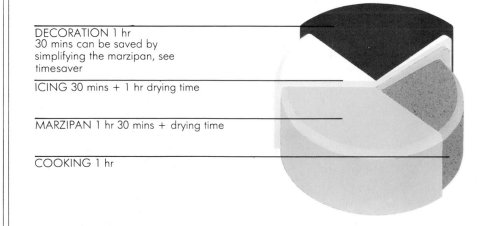

DECORATION 1 hr
30 mins can be saved by simplifying the marzipan, see timesaver

ICING 30 mins + 1 hr drying time

MARZIPAN 1 hr 30 mins + drying time

COOKING 1 hr

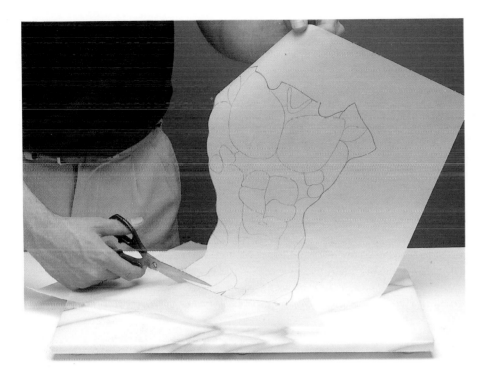

1 Using the design on *p. 188*, trace the outline and details of the muscles on a piece of grease-proof paper or cooking parchment. Cut out the design.

2 Place the paper outline on top of the cake and cut around.

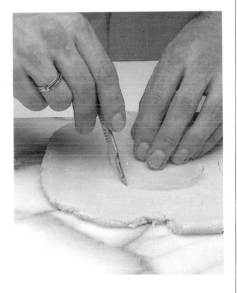

3 If it is not possible to cut out the entire shape from the cake in one go, simply reassemble the cut-off pieces and complete the cutting as in the illustration.

4 Measure the depth of the cake. Roll out a little of the marzipan and cut out one or more strips to the depth of the cake. Brush the marzipan with apricot jam and fix to the side of the cake. Continue until the sides are completely covered with marzipan. Cut out the chest muscles from the traced design. Roll out a little marzipan fairly thickly and cut around the paper guide.

5 Press the edges of the marzipan pieces to round off the cut edges.

7 Reassemble all the prepared pieces as in a jigsaw.

6 Continue cutting individual muscles and the shape of the trunks from the traced design. Roll out the marzipan and continue cutting round the shapes in turn. Gently round off all the cut edges. For complete authenticity, make the chest muscles thicker than the stomach muscles, and the stomach muscles thicker than those around the waist.

8 Spread the surface of the cake with apricot jam and position the jigsaw of marzipan pieces on the cake. Allow to dry for several hours.

9 Roll out the fondant icing on a work surface lightly dusted with cornflour. Cover the cake in one piece and gently smooth the icing over the muscles and down around the sides. Trim off the excess icing with a sharp knife. Leave to dry for an hour or so.

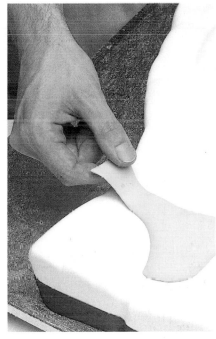

11 Cut out the icing swimming trunks using the appropriate shape on the paper design. Lay them in position on the cake.

10 Take a coloured ribbon and fix to the side of the cake with royal icing at intervals.

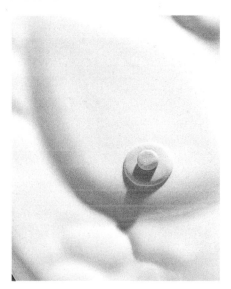

12 Roll out the dark flesh coloured icing and make the nipples. Moisten the icing with a little water and place the nipples on the chest.

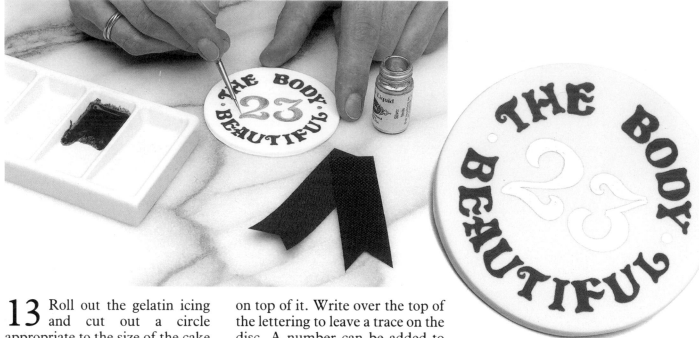

13 Roll out the gelatin icing and cut out a circle appropriate to the size of the cake and the required message. Allow to dry. Trace the 'Body Beautiful' lettering or another appropriate message (*see p.185*) on to a piece of greaseproof or tracing paper. Put a piece of graphite paper over the icing disc and lay the tracing paper on top of it. Write over the top of the lettering to leave a trace on the disc. A number can be added to the decoration if the cake is being given to celebrate a birthday, or the recipient's placing in an athletics, fitness or body-building event. Paint over the design on the disc, which can eventually be kept as a reminder of the event.

15 Fix the icing disc to the ribbon at the hip of the body with a little royal icing.

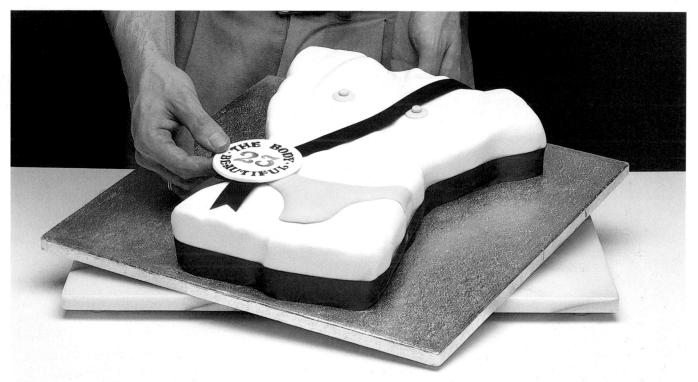

14 Cut a length of ribbon and two shorter pieces as shown and fix across the cake with a little royal icing.

CLUB COLOURS

A 9" (23cm) round carrot cake has been transformed into a prize-winner's rosette (see p. 169). This bold design is one of the simplest in the book, with the ribbon pieces cut individually from coloured icing. They can be taken off the cake before it is cut and reassembled to be kept as a reminder of the occasion. The colours of the rosette can be chosen to match those of the recipient's school, college or club.

To make the cake. Sift together the flour, baking powder, bicarbonate of soda, salt and cinnamon. Combine the walnuts and sugar in a bowl and add the eggs. Mix well. Add the melted butter and gently fold in the flour mixture until well incorporated. Mix in the grated carrot. Grease a 9" (23cm) round cake tin and line with greaseproof paper. Pour the mixture into the tin and level off the surface. Bake in a preheated oven at 180°C/350°F/Gas mark 4 for approximately 1 hour or until firm to the touch. Turn out on to a wire rack to cool.

For the filling, mix the curd cheese until softened, adding a little milk if necessary. Sweeten, flavour with the vanilla and spread on the split cake.

TIMESAVERS

DECORATION 1 hr 30 mins +
12 hrs drying time

ICING 25 mins + drying time

MARZIPAN 30 mins

COOKING 1 hr

(see p. 169)

INGREDIENTS

Cake
9oz (250g) plain flour
2 teaspoons baking powder
1 teaspoon bicarbonate of soda
½ teaspoon salt
1 teaspoon cinnamon
4oz (125g) chopped walnuts
8oz (225g) soft brown sugar
3 eggs
4oz (125g) melted butter or margarine
8oz (225g) grated raw carrot

Filling
12oz (350g) curd cheese
icing sugar to taste
vanilla flavouring

Decoration
one 12" (30cm) round cake board
1lb (450g) marzipan
1lb (450g) fondant icing
1¼lb (575g) gelatin icing
apricot jam
a little royal icing

Equipment
food colour
ribbon

1 Cut the cake in half and sandwich together with the filling.

3 On a work surface lightly dusted with cornflour roll out the fondant icing into a circle large

enough to cover the cake. Lay the icing over the cake and press into the edges. Using a large flat-

2 On a work surface lightly dusted with icing sugar, roll out 8oz (225g) of the marzipan. Take the tin in which the cake was baked and using the base as a guide cut out a circle of marzipan. Spread the top of the cake with apricot jam and fix the marzipan to the top of the cake. Using a piece of string or cotton measure the circumference of the cake, and also measure its depth. Roll out the remaining 8oz (225g) marzipan and cut out one or two strips according to the measurements taken. Spread the sides of the cake with apricot jam and fix the marzipan on to the cake.

bladed knife held against the sides of the cake, trim off any excess icing and allow to dry for several hours.

6 When the icing is dry trace out the '21' using the numbers on *p. 185*. Transfer the number to the centre of the rosette using graphite paper. Paint the number blue and leave to dry.

4 Take the gelatin icing and colour half of it blue and the other half yellow. Using the designs on *p. 189* trace out the shapes that make up the ribbon to go round the top of the cake and the tail pieces that extend from its edge. Roll out the blue icing and cut out 8 of the ribbon sections.

ASSEMBLY

Wrap the silk ribbon round the edge of the cake and fix with a little royal icing. Place the icing ribbon sections around the top of the cake, alternating the blue and yellow pieces. When evenly spaced, place the rosette centre in the middle. Finally, insert the two tail pieces under the ribbon edging. If the cake is to be transported any distance the individual pieces can be fixed to it with royal icing. Otherwise the pieces are best left loose so that they can be removed and the cake evenly sliced.

5 Cut out one tail piece in blue. Repeat using the yellow icing and cut an additional circular piece for the centre of the rosette measuring about 4″ (10cm) in diameter – a saucer will provide a good cutting guide. Allow the pieces to dry for about 12 hours. Turn each piece over after several hours so that the air gets to both sides.

THATCHED COTTAGE

Four 8" (20cm) square fruit cakes need only simple carving to transform them into a charming country cottage (see p.173). We have used royal icing here instead of fondant, just to show how simply a professional finish can be achieved. The finishing touches are provided by careful hand painting of the thatch and brickwork and a colourful display of country garden flowers.

To make the cake. Mix together the flour, cake crumbs, baking powder and sugar. Rub in the butter or margarine. Beat the eggs with 6floz (180ml) milk. Add to the flour mixture with the fruit and beat thoroughly until mixed. The mixture should be of soft dropping consistency. Add the remaining milk if necessary. Turn the mixture into a greased and lined 8" (20cm) square cake tin and bake in a preheated oven at 180°C/350°F/Gas mark 4 for 1 hour 15 minutes or until golden and firm to the touch. Turn out and allow to cool on a wire rack.

INGREDIENTS

(for one cake)
8 oz (225g) wholemeal flour
8oz (225g) cake crumbs
4 teaspoons baking powder
8oz (225g) demerara sugar
4oz (125g) butter or margarine
4 eggs
8floz (240ml) milk
12oz (350g) dried mixed fruit

Decoration
12" (30cm) square cake board
royal icing made with 4 egg whites
2lb (900g) marzipan
apricot jam

Equipment
food colour
lustre powder

TIMESAVERS

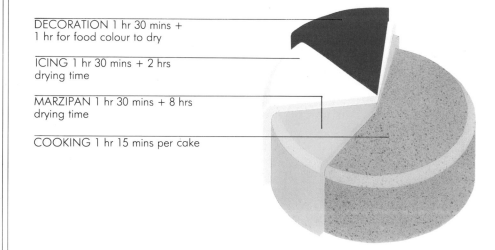

DECORATION 1 hr 30 mins +
1 hr for food colour to dry

ICING 1 hr 30 mins + 2 hrs
drying time

MARZIPAN 1 hr 30 mins + 8 hrs
drying time

COOKING 1 hr 15 mins per cake

1 Pile the cakes on top of each other.

2 Use the layers of cake to help you plan the carving of the cottage. Look at all the illustrations before you begin and study the relationship of the individual features to each other and their position on the block of cake. To start carving the roof take a sharp kitchen knife and draw a line across the top of the cake to divide it in half. This line will be the highest point of the roof. Note that the front of the roof features a window extending out from under the thatch. You will need to mark out the window before you cut the roof. Take a knife and draw a 2″ (5cm) square on the third layer beginning 2″ (5cm) in from the right wall. On the right-hand wall mark a line with the knife from the mid-point line drawn on the top cake, to the top of the second layer. Begin cutting the top cake 2″ (5cm) in from the right wall using the slanting line just drawn as a guide, thereby shaping the roof up to the edge of the window. Returning to the top of the cake, cut another 2″ (5cm) section fol-

lowing the same slanting line as before, but this time stopping half way down the roof. Moving to the front of the cake, cut a line into the cake along the top of the square that marks out the window, cutting about 1½″ (4cm) back into the cake. This line should meet up with the slanting line just carved and expose the top of the window. Before carving out the remaining section of the front of the thatched roof, it is important to mark out the chimney.

3 The chimney is 2″ (5cm) wide and is carved into the left wall. With the point of the knife, score two vertical lines 2″ (5cm) apart into the end of the cake, that is one line 3″ (7.5cm) in from each corner. Leave this 2″ (5cm) piece intact but cut ¾″ (2cm) into the wall on either side to expose the chimney breast. Returning to the top of the cake, take a point 2″ (5cm) in from the chimney breast and cut a slanting line down towards the left wall ending at the top of the second layer. Obviously you will have to cut around the chimney in order to leave it intact. Cut the remaining section of the front of the roof to expose the window completely. Cut the roof at the back of the cottage to match the angle of the front roof – there is no window here.

4 One additional feature needs to be carved before continuing. Cut out a 1″ (2.5cm) square block from the front left-hand corner of the cake from the board up to the top of the second layer under the roof. This will eventually be the log stove. To produce an overhanging thatched roof, carefully trim away about ¼″ (5mm) from all the walls. Trim away all straight lines and edges on the roof to produce a rounded thatch.

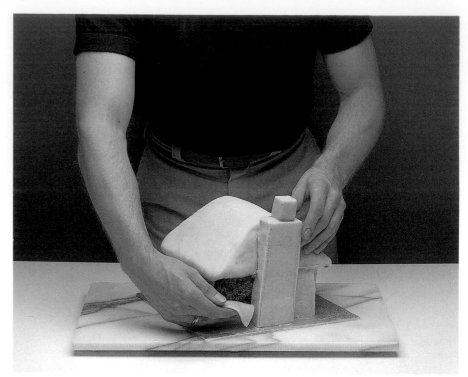

5 Any irregularities in the marzipanning of this cake will be hidden under the royal icing. However, try to be as neat as possible. Before marzipanning each section measure it and cut a piece of marzipan to fit. Spread the cake with apricot jam and fix on the marzipan.

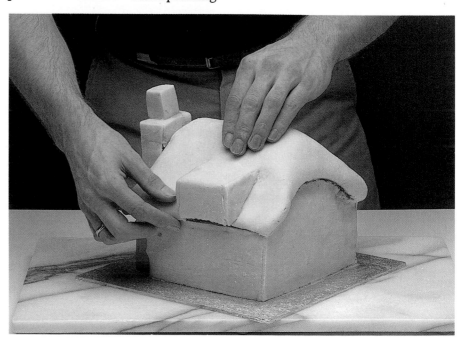

6 Cut a block of marzipan about 1″ (2.5cm) high to stick on top of the chimney for extra height. Stick it on with royal icing. Smooth the surfaces and press the seams together with your fingers to give the cake a rounded appearance. Allow to dry for eight hours or overnight.

7 The royal icing used to cover this cake should be stiff but spreadable. If the icing is too soft, the detail you score into the surface will not hold. Moisten the marzipan with water to make it sticky. Smooth the icing on to the cake with an ordinary kitchen knife or a small spatula. It is a good idea to ice the cake one section at a time, beginning with the roof. The detail should be scored into the wet icing and then left to dry. Make the surface of the icing as regular as possible. If it is not smooth, try dipping your knife into lukewarm water and smoothing it again. You could also do this with a wet finger – in fact all the icing could be applied by hand if you prefer.

8 When one section is completely iced take a bamboo skewer or cocktail stick and score in the detail. On the roof, score fine vertical lines from top to bottom of the thatch except for two decorative bands as illustrated. Elsewhere, score in details on the windows, door, log stove and beams. When the cake is fully iced allow to dry for two hours.

To make bushes and climbing flowers around the cottage, pile royal icing on the board and against the walls and prick all over with a skewer to make the surface rough. Leave to dry for an hour, then paint in various shades of green, leaving white spaces for the flowers that can be touched in with colour later, as it is difficult to apply colour effectively to a dark green surface. The flowers on the bushes were dabbed thickly with lustre powder. (Note that lustre powder does not stick evenly to vertical surfaces.) Finally, if you wish, lightly dust the thatched roof with gold lustre powder for a magical finish.

9 Paint the cake with a number of food colours. The colour will collect in the scored lines, giving the illusion of texture and depth.

10 Several shades can be brushed into each other on the chimney and the thatch to produce a weathered effect. Do not overload your brush when painting the beams in case the colour drips down and spoils the effect.

LADY LIBERTY

The jaded figure of beautiful Lady Liberty reclines after a gruelling night on the tiles on a couch of orange marmalade cake (made out of a 12″/30cm square) draped in the Stars and Stripes. Liberty's body is sculpted out of white marzipan and her shades are made of thin card. Her jewels are diamanté. *This cake is bound to inspire you with other ideas for portraying the famous at leisure.*

To make the cake. Grease a 12″ (30cm) square tin and line with greaseproof paper. Sift the flour and spices together. Cream the butter or margarine with the sugar and orange rind until light and fluffy. Beat in the eggs two at a time followed by one tablespoon flour after each addition. Fold in the marmalade followed by the remaining flour, orange juice and milk. Spoon the mixture into the prepared tin and level the top. Bake in a preheated oven at 160°C/325°F/Gas mark 3 for 1¼–1½ hours. The cake is ready when risen and firm to the touch. Leave it in the tin for a few minutes, then turn out to cool on a wire rack.

For the filling, cream the butter or margarine and icing sugar. Mix in the marmalade and orange juice and use to sandwich the pieces of cake together.

Cake
1lb (450g) self-raising flour
2 teaspoons ground mixed spice
12oz (350g) butter or margarine
12oz (350g) soft brown sugar
grated rind and juice of 2 oranges
6 eggs
4 tablespoons chunky orange marmalade
4 tablespoons milk

Filling
4oz (125g) butter or margarine
12oz (350g) sifted icing sugar
2 tablespoons marmalade
1 tablespoon orange juice

Decoration
14″ (35cm) round cake board
1½lb (675g) yellow marzipan
1 ¼lb (575g) white marzipan
2lb (900g) fondant icing
apricot jam
royal icing

Equipment
food colour
thin card
diamanté

TIMESAVERS

DECORATION 3 hrs + 6 hrs drying time
45 mins can be cut from the decoration time by using the Timesavers

ICING 30 mins + 6 hrs drying time

MARZIPAN 40 mins + 1 hr drying time

COOKING 1 hr 30 mins

2 Using a sharp kitchen knife cut the smaller piece of cake in half on the diagonal. Enjoy the offcut of cake with a cup of tea.

1 Cut the cake into three rectangles 12″ × 4″ (30 × 10cm). Using three quarters of the filling, sandwich two of the pieces together. Cut the remaining piece into two rectangles 4″ × 3″ (10 × 7.5cm). Use the remaining filling to sandwich these two pieces together as illustrated.

3 The front edge, top and back of the cake form three rectangles each measuring 4″ (10cm) in width. To marzipan the cake measure the length of each of these three rectangles. Spread the surfaces with apricot jam. Roll out half the yellow marzipan and cut out three pieces to the measurements just noted. Fix the first piece to the front of the cake. The second covers the top of the lounger and extends up the inclined back. The third piece covers the back of the lounger. To marzipan the sides, hold a piece of greaseproof or tracing paper against the cake and lightly trace out the shape. Cut a rectangle and a triangle of marzipan to fit. Spread the sides of the cake with apricot jam and fix the pieces in position. Allow the marzipan to dry for an hour or so before proceeding.

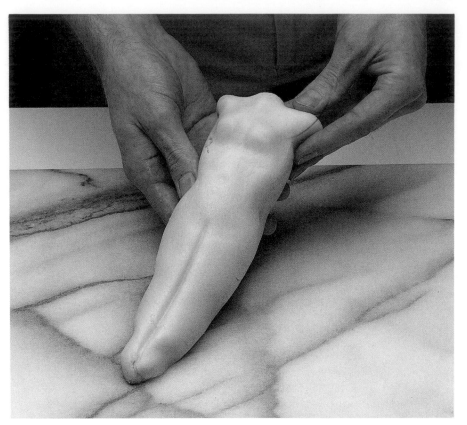

4 Setting 4oz (125g) fondant icing aside, roll out the rest into a large rectangle on a work surface lightly dusted with corn flour. The piece should be large enough to cover the whole cake and drape decoratively at the corners. Lay the icing over the cake and arrange the folds. Allow to dry for six hours. Trace the design for the stars and stripes from *p.190*. Hold the tracing against the side of the cake and gently score the pattern into the icing. Be very careful not to press too hard, or you could break the icing sheet or the folds. Draw the stars freehand to prevent this if necessary. Paint the background stripe midnight blue, leaving the stars white. Let the blue colour dry for an hour, then paint the Christmas red stripes. Leave to dry while moulding Lady Liberty.

5 To mould the body roll out 1lb (450g) white marzipan into a cylindrical shape tapering slightly towards one end. Pinch the wide end of the piece to make a neck and shoulders. Gently pinch the cylinder a third of the way along to make a waist, then begin to mould the hips, thighs, calves and ankles. Mould the breasts. It is not necessary to mould detail for the feet as Liberty is wearing shoes. Score a line into the marzipan to indicate the separation of the two legs.

TIPS

Painting the stars and stripes on the flag is quite time-consuming. You could colour the icing by kneading red into it before you roll it out and buy a small paper or silk Stars and Stripes – perhaps even two of them – to anchor in the cake above the lady's head.

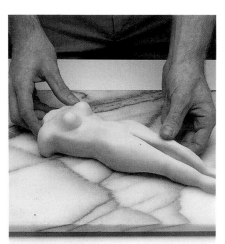

6 With a sharp knife, cut along the line dividing the legs, then round off the cut edges to make them shapely. Put the finishing touches to the body moulding and lay the body in position on the surface of the cake, taking care to leave enough room for the head. If you want one knee bent, support it underneath with the end of a pencil until the marzipan has dried in position, then remove it.

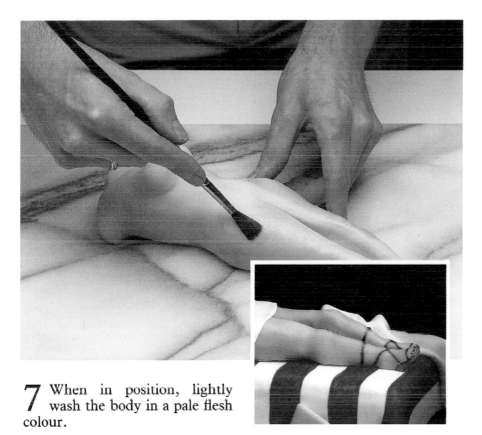

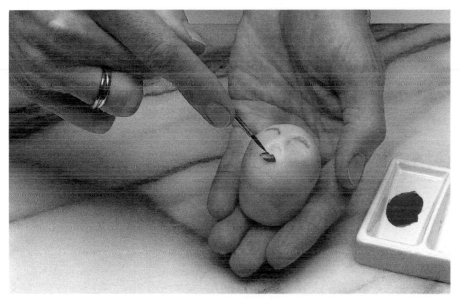

7 When in position, lightly wash the body in a pale flesh colour.

8 To make the head take 1oz (25g) white marzipan and roll into a ball. Press the ball to elongate it slightly and produce a chin. Gently pinch up a small nose and press a fingertip into the marzipan at either side of it to make the eye sockets. With a cocktail stick lightly score in a hairline. Lightly wash the head in a pale flesh colour except for the hair, which should be golden. If you wish, add a little more colour at the cheekbones for emphasis. When the wash is dry, paint in the eyebrows and lips. Place the head in position on the body, fixing the two parts together with royal icing.

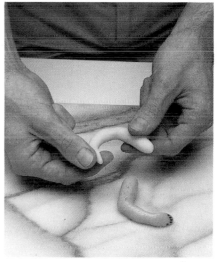

9 To make the arms take 1oz (25g) white marzipan and roll into two sausage shapes about 2½″ (6.5cm) long. Bend in two places for the elbow and wrist and pinch to make a hand. Wash in pale flesh colour and pick out the nails in Christmas red. Allow to dry for an hour. When dry, fix the arm that stretches up and behind the head in position, fixing it to the body with a dab of royal icing. Do not place the other arm in position yet.

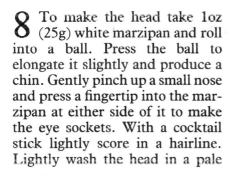

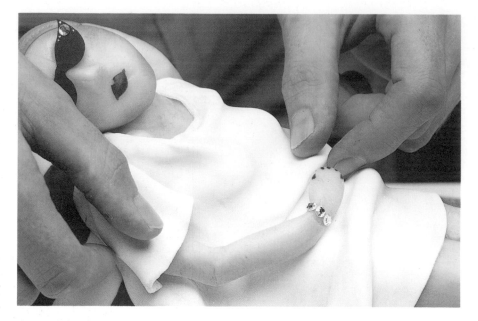

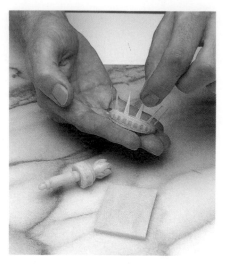

10 Take the remaining 4oz (125g) fondant icing and colour a pale peppermint shade. Roll out thinly and cut out a 3" (7.5cm) square. Arrange the icing round the neck of the statue and drape decoratively over the body. When this piece of icing is in position fix the second arm across the body with a dab of royal icing at the shoulder. Cut out a small triangular piece from the leftover peppermint icing and arrange over the shoulder to make a sleeve. Keep any leftovers. Cut the sunglasses from thin card and paint with black food colour. Add tiny pieces of *diamanté* and silver food colour for further effect. Use *diamanté* too to make a bracelet.

12 To make the regalia take 2oz (50g) white marzipan and mould as illustrated. The points of the crown are made from thin pieces of card. Brush with peppermint food colour to match the clothing.

ASSEMBLY

Paint further washes of peppermint on to the clothing to add more definition if you wish. Roll out any peppermint icing leftovers and drape over the corner of the lounger to represent discarded layers of clothing. Arrange the regalia. For a truly glamorous effect decorate the edge of the board with *diamanté*.

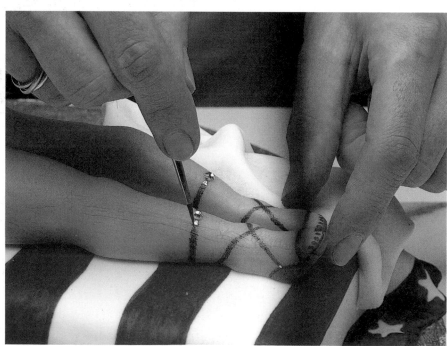

11 To finish the feet, paint on the detail of the shoes and paint the toenails Christmas red. Add small pieces of *diamanté* for glamour.

ABCDEFGHIJKLMNOPQRSTUVWXYZ

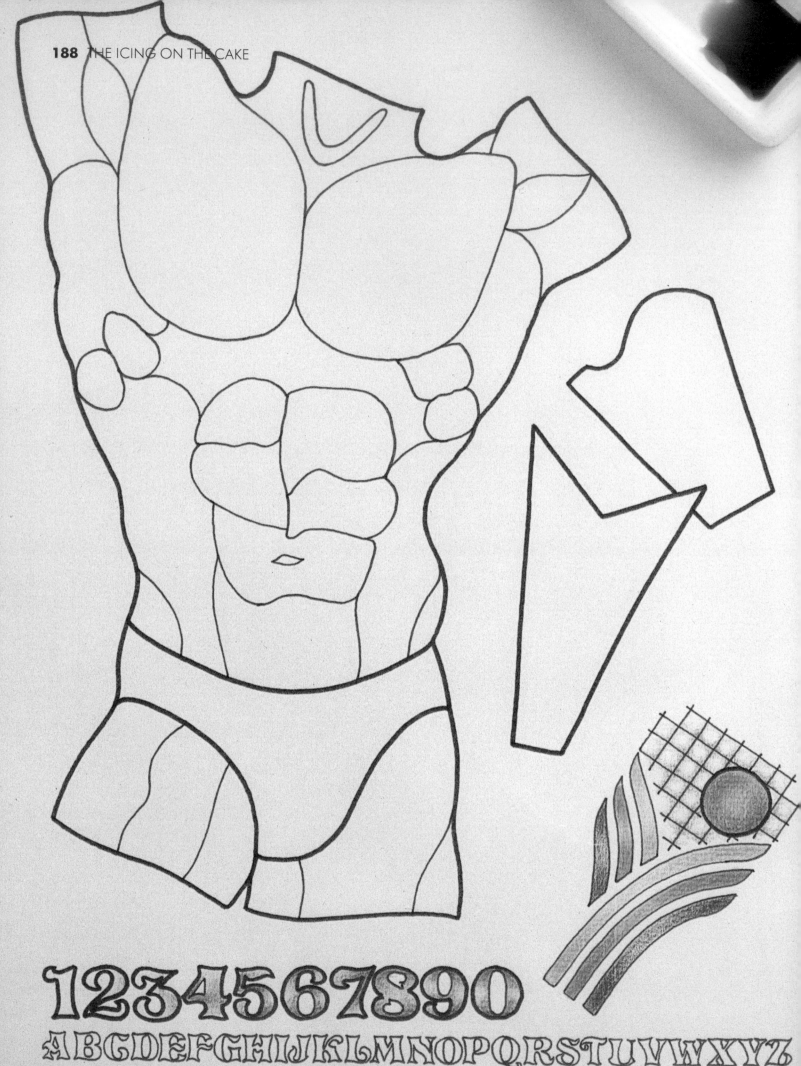

With Love
x

SUPPLIERS

**F & P CATERING
SERVICES LTD**
*81 Hoe Street
WalthamstowLondon E17
tel (081) 520 0893
Personal shoppers, mail
order, tuition and
demonstration*

HOMEBAKERS SUPPLIES
*157-159 High Street
Wolstanton
Newcastle
Staffs ST5 0EJ
tel (0782) 614119
Personal shoppers,
mail order*

SQUIRE'S KITCHEN
*Squire's House
3 Waverley Lane
Farnham
Surrey GU9 8BB
tel (0252) 711749/734309
Personal shoppers, mail
order, courses*

WOODNUTTS
*97 Church Road
Hove
Sussex BN3 2BA
tel (0273) 205353
School, demonstration,
personal shoppers and
mail order*

**CAKECRAFT ARTISTRY
AND SUNDRIES**
*65 Gales Drive
Three Bridges
Crawley
Sussex RH10 1QA
tel (0293) 520875
Personal shoppers,
demonstration*

**MARY FORD CAKE
ARTISTRY CENTRE**
*28-30 Southbourne Grove
Southbourne
Bournemouth
Dorset BH6 3RA
tel (0202) 422 653
Mail order, personal
shoppers, tuition and
demonstration*

THE FINISHING TOUCH
*17 St Patrick's Square
Edinburgh
Scotland EH8 9EZ
tel (031) 667 0914
Personal shoppers, some
mail order*

**THE CAKE AND
CHOCOLATE SHOP**
*12 Bruntsfield Place
Edinburgh
Scotland EH10 4HN
tel (031) 228 4350
Tuition and retail*

**B R MATTHEWS AND
SONS**
*12 Gipsy Hill
London SE19 1NN
tel (081) 670 0788
Personal shoppers, mail
order, tuition*

CRUMBS OF LONDON
*12 Methuen Park
London N10 2YS
tel (081) 444 0393
Personal commissions,
tuition*

This is a list of only some of the suppliers around the country. For more information and addresses in your area you could contact:

**THE SUGARCRAFT
GUILD**
*Wellington House
Messiter Place
Eltham
London SE9 5DP
tel (081) 859 6943*

ACKNOWLEDGEMENTS

Greg Robinson and Max Schofield would like to thank Linda Sonntag for her help in editing the book and Mark French for his beautiful photography. Thanks also to Lou Segal and Julia Burns of Frederick's Restaurant, London N1 for their help and support during the production of the book, and most importantly to Nigel Osborne for his endless patience, encouragement and friendship.

Special thanks to Ray Jaeggi for the loan of equipment photographed in the book.